"Reading Lenay's book is like sitting ... ... write grandmother. Lenay gives real life examples of how she moved through her own grief process. With her gentle style and comforting touch, readers will feel surrounded by love and get in touch with their own inner strength as they go through the journey. I wish I had Lenay's book during the time after my mom died, it would've made a real difference."

— Jennifer Coken, Author, *When I Die, Take My Panties: Turning Your Darkest Moments into Your Greatest Gifts.*

"One day each of us will need a shoulder to cry on and a soothing voice to comfort our pain. Even though there is no one shoe that fits all when it comes to grieving the loss of a friend or loved one, Lenay's book, ***Grief Comfort Guide,*** will help anyone who is going through the grieving process. Through her personal experiences of coping with and overcoming the loss of so many loved ones, she has provided a detailed guide in her book of how each one of us can better cope with grief."

— Lena McCalla-Njee, MA, Special Education, author of *Autism Inspires* and *Ivan Gets a Dream House,*

"I thought your 10 ways to handle grief an excellent guide. What I really liked about your book is that it's person to person and not theory on how to handle grief; it's a layman's guide without all the psychoanalysis. It's something that the everyday person will be able to understand and relate to and be helped by because its solutions are real world and commonsense. Good for you. And I think everyone will be able to recognize themselves and their feelings in this book. I guess what I'm trying to say is that it's honest."

— Madalyn Stone, Editor

Grief Comfort Guide

A Personal Journey from Loss to Light

They Were Here. They Did Exist. They Mattered.

Marie Lenay Rogus

Copyright © 2017 by Marie Rogus

Twilight Garden Publishing
San Marcos, California

All rights reserved. No part of this book may be reproduced by any mechanical, photographic, or electronic process, or in the form of a phonographic recording; nor may it be stored in a retrieval system, transmitted, or otherwise be copied for public or private use—other than for "fair use" as brief quotations embodied in articles and reviews without prior written permission of the publisher.

Library of Congress Control Number: 2017902766

ISBN: 978-0-9985249-0-0 (Print)

ISBN: 978-0-9985249-1-7 (E-Book)

Acknowledgments

I would like to thank my husband John for believing in me and giving me the courage to write this book and to my daughter Nichole who went through all this with me and gave me her encouragement and love.

Also, I want to thank Dan MacDougall and Laurie Cain who believed in me and read my manuscript, and to my Ya Ya sisters Joellen, Jen, and Sholita who encouraged me and kept me going and to my editor, Madalyn Stone and Deana Riddle who guided me through the publishing process.

I also want to express my deep gratitude to Martha Bullen, my conductor, and to all of my Quantum Leap Coaches. You are the best!

— Marie Lenay Rogus

Table of Contents

Life Interrupted

I was afraid, trembling, cold, and eight-months pregnant as I walked down the hospital hall. A tang of disinfectant was in the air, and I could hear the echo of my footsteps. My senses were so heightened. I walked into my husband's room and stopped in horror.

It registered in my mind that Jack was sitting up in the bed, but my attention was riveted on the ominous machine in the middle of the room. There was a nurse with scissors in her hand ready to cut at what seemed to be yards of blood-filled plastic tubing.

I thought, "My God, what is she doing? Jack is hooked up to those tubes!"

The machine looked like a terrible monster, menacing with blood tubes running everywhere and ending in Jack's arm. Sitting in the middle of this five-foot-tall thing was a fiber coil filled with his blood that was submerged in a vessel of liquid just like the brains you see in horror films. It was like something from a *Frankenstein* movie, and I thought all of Jack's blood was in the kidney dialysis machine.

Once I calmed down, I learned there were only a couple pints of blood in the machine, and the "scissors" were a hemostat that was used to clamp the tubes.

After that moment of terror, I saw that Jack was sitting up and in a pretty good mood, considering. I kissed him and joked that this was a funny way to get my attention. We talked more about what was going on. Then he suddenly threw up and passed out. Alarms sounded everywhere, doctors came running, and a nurse pushed me back into a corner. I hit the wall behind me and stopped breathing…

Part I
Grief

Chapter 1
Grief Happens to All of Us

Deep grief is unbearable, agonizing. I wanted to speak with someone who knew what I was feeling but didn't know anyone who could help. I didn't know how I could get through the emotional pain, or if I could. I felt as though a large tree trunk had been ripped from my chest, leaving an invisible, gaping hole with my lifeblood leaking on the ground...but no one could see it.

There wasn't a road map that told me how to deal with my grief, so I made a lot of mistakes that hurt me, and I learned over time what I could do to make myself feel a bit better. I decided to share how I coped with the grief of losing seven of my loved ones, so I've written their stories to bring them to life, and I've put together this guide with suggestions that helped me. I hope you will find some comfort in them. Writing about my loved ones was very hard, but saying their names and talking about incidents that I remembered helped heal my spirit as I rejoiced in their memory. *They were here. They did exist. They mattered.*

If you are reading this book, you may have recently lost a loved one, and you're looking for answers, inspiration, and some kind of meaning that will allow you to go on. I know I was. I looked at all of the grief and life-after-death books I could find. I wanted to know if my loved one was alright wherever he or she was. I needed to know.

This book is a bit different from many of the books on grief that are available. It may seem a little heavy—and I'm sorry about that—but your heart is also probably very heavy now as you try to find some solace. I don't write about what grief is on an intellectual basis or about the various stages of grief. Instead, this guide is about *my* experience with grief, what I've encountered, and how I got through it. Many books may try to give you answers—not this one. I will share my experience with the process and the tortured healing. Perhaps by sharing my journey toward healing, you may read something that can help you as well. Stay away from negative self-talk. You can and will get through this. It will take time, but you can heal. You *will* feel joy and happiness again.

Chapter 2

When Faith and Grief Intersect

Grief has no religion. It comes to all of us. I spoke to a woman who gave birth to twin baby girls; the girls died shortly after they were born. "Why would you take my beautiful girls, God?" she asked. She was so angry and agonized by her grief that she temporarily lost her faith. As with the story of Job in the Bible, we have so much emotional pain, we feel we have been forgotten and forsaken.

My personal belief is that we are all magnificent, spiritual beings having human experiences with their joys and challenges. The challenges forge us into remembering who we really are. The loss of loved ones has spurred people to erect magnificent buildings, hospitals, and do other things—something—they needed to do to honor the memory of those they lost, which can bring good to so many others. Their actions emphasized that their lost loved ones were here.

Having a spiritual faith definitely can help you heal. It helped me. No matter if you reach for God, Jesus Christ, Allah, Buddha, a Higher Power, Supreme Being, Nature, or Mother Earth and Father Sky, going inside yourself and finding that presence can bring you some peace.

After losing my loved ones, I learned to dig deep down inside myself and find the Presence within me that made me feel I was not alone, that I had the ingrained strength to go on and not only regain my life, but live it fully and realize that the grieving gave me something intangible. It let me touch an awareness of more, of something greater than myself.

Faith is important to help you heal. But if faith in God isn't your belief, find somewhere to be at peace. Find something grander than yourself, something majestic. Find others through groups or online forums. Knowing others feel as you do may help you get through one more day. And what you share may help someone else as well.

Chapter 3

Finding My Own Faith

After a lot of self-contemplation, I decided to share my faith and belief system with you. I want you to know that I respect all faiths. I do believe there are more paths to God then we can ever know. I believe that we are all hosts to our Divine Creator, Supreme Being, in our minds— that we are all part of the vast Intelligence of the Universe.

Please believe me when I say that I honor your religious beliefs whatever they are, and I hope that what I say about mine won't prejudice you against this book and the healing that can take place. This is just part of my journey.

I was baptized Lutheran but never remembered Mom taking me to church. Our home was filled with prayers from my grandmother, who was Serbian Orthodox. When I was twelve years old, a woman took me under her care. Her name was Marian, and she was a Jehovah's Witness. She came by the house one day and decided I was her priority. Mom was okay with it. She felt Marian had a good heart and wouldn't harm me. The Jehovah's Witnesses were wonderful, kind people. But they didn't tolerate any other ideologies other than their own and ostracized those who left their circle.

When I was sixteen, I decided that it didn't make sense to me that I had to knock on doors to get into Heaven. It seemed to me that if I loved God, I would automatically be welcomed Home. But that wasn't the belief of the Jehovah's Witnesses, so I left. It wasn't easy for me as I was connected to their beliefs and felt I would never get to Heaven now. But my inner strength took hold after a while, and I knew I'd made the right decision. Never again would I be narrow-minded about anything.

I went to many Christian churches to find the right one, but I'm a free spirit with beliefs that I've gathered over time and after much reading. When I got married I converted to Judaism, but after Jack's death I didn't know enough to continue, and in my thirties, I

9

found the Church of Religious Science, or Science of Mind. It was metaphysical, and I felt that I had come home. I think my desire to become a hypnotherapist came from the study of the mind and stemmed from what I learned of how the mind works. Finally, I had found a group that felt as I did. I learned to meditate and felt that the Divine Spirit would always be by my side. Then I read the *Course in Miracles* and discovered myself and my current beliefs.

I believe in Peace and Love. I don't judge others. I accept all beliefs. Our belief systems may vary, but the bottom line is, "Do unto others as you would have them do unto you." Let's love one another and choose to see Peace in this moment.

As grief visited me, I called upon the Divine within me to help me because by myself, I can do nothing.

My feelings about grief have changed over time as each family member died. This is why I wanted to share my journey with you. My hope is that you will read something that will give you the encouragement you need to help you get through your own grief.

Chapter 4

Grief Takes Us on a Wild Ride

Sadly, while I was writing this book, my daughter called, and barely able to get the words out, told me my son-in-law had died suddenly of a massive heart attack at work. Russ Miller and my daughter, Nichole, had only been married ten months, and they were very happy and looking forward to starting a family. After I heard that he had died, and I told her my husband and I were on our way to her, I hung up and really lost it. I screamed and yelled and cried while my husband drove the twenty-five minutes to their home. It took me that long to calm down. The loss of my daughter's happiness was unbearable for me. That lost, clouded look, the inexpressible sadness in her eyes was so hard to see.

When I lost my husband Jack, I was the lost one. I came home to the loneliness of an empty home and tried to understand how someone can just "disappear." It's impossible to comprehend, impossible to bear, yet I went on, putting one foot in front of the other, tears in my eyes with a heavy heart even though something major was missing in my life—the companionship, the hugs and kisses good night, the cuddling in bed. That snuggling and cuddling is so wonderful, but now it was gone. The bed was empty and cold.

When a deep wave of grief hits, it turns you inside out. Sometimes, the wave is so bad, you think you cannot go on. Fortunately, the wave doesn›t last long, but when it has you in its grip, you have no control. The best thing you can do is hold onto something as it rips through you. It helps if you can have someone you love hold you close until it's over. Going through it by yourself is intolerable. But you do it. The wave does pass even as it wrings you out.

Cry, scream, give in to your grief as long as you need to because that is the only way you will heal. If you don't allow yourself to feel your grief, it will come out in other far more dangerous ways. Depression, panic attacks, and illness can result from trying to ignore or suppress grief. You cannot run away from grief or pretend it isn't there. Being stoic doesn't work either because the underlying grief will go inside, incubate, and surface later in ways that can be destructive.

And just when you start to feel a bit stable, a large wave of grief turns you over inside like a riptide. It can happen anywhere, anytime, and at the most inconvenient times. You may be in a supermarket and see a food that reminds you of your loved one. That happened to me. I saw my son's favorite chili and lost it. I felt like screaming and almost fell to my knees. I ran out of the store to my car and sat there yelling and sobbing. I knew that in time it would pass. I'd get through it. It takes time…a lot of time, but you will get through it, too.

In days past, it was normal to wear black during the one-year period of mourning. It does take that long to get your bearings even though you may still be in somewhat of a mental fog. I look back and realize that I was in a fog for a long time after my son died, and I don't remember much of what I did during that time. It took me two years to come out of severe grief after my husband Jack died, and I had just met my current husband, John. But I would still break out in a wave of grief and start to cry. I remember it happened when John was standing with me in the kitchen. He just held me close and told me he had another shoulder on his other side to cry on if I needed it. What a guy. No wonder I kept him.

Many experts say no major decisions should be made for at least one year when you are grieving. That isn't always easy to do if you have to move because you cannot pay the rent or mortgage on your own. Some decisions must be made. Find family or others who you trust to advise you because you may be afraid of making a wrong decision because you can't think clearly. I made the mistake of listening to the wrong people and lost money in the stock market. I learned the hard way that if you are going to invest in something, do the research and learn all about it. Wait until you are ready.

Also, you can have moments of what I call "the Crazies." A couple of months after my son died, I was standing in an aisle at the supermarket with my current husband. He must have said he needed to use the bathroom, but I didn't hear him as I was studying a food label. When I realized he was gone, I got "the Crazies." I put my feet apart to brace my stance, and then started to go over it in my mind. "I know I came in with John. I remember him driving me here. I'm not really alone." And all the while I'm trying not to panic. I stood like that, absolutely still, thinking madly until he returned and I got my breath back.

Another aspect about grief is that when someone you love dies, you think about everyone else you have loved who passed away, which compounds your grief. You feel the passing of all those who have gone before. They dance around in your head.

I found it difficult to deal with someone else's grief. I knew how to experience grief myself but didn't know how to console my friend during her loss. It surprised me that I felt awkward. Then I reached into my own experience and realized that you really cannot console anyone trying to get through the death of a loved one. I told her that I loved her and was there for her. But she wanted isolation and didn't open one condolence card. That was how she coped.

The shock of a death can last up to a week or so. But you can help your friend or family member by offering to babysit, to bring a meal by, to do the laundry, or just make that telephone call once a week. Don't ask how they are because they will just say they are okay. Ask if they are eating or sleeping properly. Ask more personal questions that don't require a yes or no answer. After a month or so, you can offer to take them to dinner or a movie, but that telephone call still helps. Being with people also helps, but those grief waves can come in public at the most inopportune times. Just, please, don't tell them to get over it and start living again. That will just make them angry, and anger is a big part of initial grief—that and *guilt*.

Did you ever notice we get lost in semantics and what is politically correct? Did he "die," "pass away," "cross over," "make her transition"? Did we "lose" him? Well, yes, all of those. Should you care? *No.* It's hard enough to say any of those words; it's especially hard to say "he died" or she's dead." It really hurts your soul. Can you get those words out without crying? Choking up? You may still choke up a year later, ten years later, maybe longer. You may happen upon an acquaintance who doesn't know of your bereavement, and that person may say, "How are your children?" or "How is your husband (wife)?" Or how about this, "How many children do you have?" How do you answer this question if you've lost a child? Even after a number of years, this is still a hard question to hear. So you numbly gloss over the answer with "two" (or however many you have) because you really don't want to get into this discussion. Then the person asks, "How old are they now?" Getting through grief is like walking through a minefield; emotional pain is waiting at every wrong step.

The other unbelievably hard word to say is "good-bye." In spite of all the well-meaning intentions of your family, friends, and religious minister, you don't have to say, "Good-bye." I firmly believe our loved ones remain close to us, and if you say something like, "Good-bye, go into the Light," you have closed off an avenue to reach beyond the grief experience. You cannot experience the "gifts" our loved ones can give us from the "other side," real or imagined.

Be aware of such gifts in the moment. I was driving down the road one day when a huge rainbow of balloons detached from a car dealership and floated right in front of my car. It was like a message to me that said, "Lighten up." Another time, I was driving in an unfamiliar area in a different town. It was twilight. As I slowed to a stop at a signal, I looked to my left, and in the same plaza I saw one neon sign that said "Millie's Diner," and another one that said "Chad's Place." This was like gifts from my sister and son—messages from beyond. At least that's how I took it, and it brought me comfort. Do you think I could ever find that place again? I don't.

This is my journey, and you don't have to agree with me. As we go on, I'll explain why I feel this way and why I feel that you can also find a measure of peace in the midst of your grief. I do have strong opinions about this subject. You will find that over time, you will, too.

Just know that you will get through this. It will take time. It takes the mind a long time to process that someone you love is no longer with you. You will find your way. Give it time—even a long time. You deserve to have a wonderful life. Don't judge yourself, but do find help, preferably with others going through what you are going through. Reach out. Don't go through this by yourself in isolation. Grief causes stress that can make you ill. Get a massage or go to a chiropractor or acupuncturist to rest your mind and heal your stress. Meditation, yoga, and hypnosis create immune-enhancing chemicals that allow you a few moments of peace and help your mind and body heal.

Chapter 5

Ten Comfort Suggestions for Easing Grief

Here are some of my personal recommendations that may bring some comfort when your loved one has just died:

1. **Get a plain, white, 7-day candle and put it in a safe place.**
   You can find them in most Catholic stores. Amazon.com has them and so does www.originalbotanica.com. After my son died, a friend of my mom's came by with a white 7-day candle in glass. She is one of the most holy women I've ever known. You just feel she was touched by God. When she gave me the candle, she told me how to use it. It was one of the most cherished items I received after Chad's death.

   I said a prayer as I lit the candle and put it on the counter near the sink in my bathroom adjoining the master bedroom, and I put a picture of Chad and something meaningful to him next to it. At night, I could see the flicker of the light on the ceiling, but the light was far enough away to let me sleep and still comfort me. It's very strange how comforting candlelight can be. I would light one candle before the next went out, and I kept it up for over a year.

2. **Find something that has been worn or used by your loved one—a shirt, sweater, pillow, and so on. NEVER WASH IT!** I found that the scent in Chad's T-shirt remained for ten years, and it was comforting. Sometimes, I wonder if it had a little "help" from beyond. It becomes your crying towel so to speak, but so what? Who cares

what you do as long as you are comforted. Holding and stroking clothes are normal. And if someone objects or tries to take an item away from you because the person mistakenly thinks it's adding to your grief, just ask that person to close the door on the way out. People like this will never understand anyway. (My goodness, I didn't realize I still had this anger in me until I started writing this paragraph.) I've had people look at me like I'm a weak person and imply that I should just get over it, that my grief had gone on long enough. How insulting!

3. **Find your Wailing Wall.** A good friend of mine, Micki, found her Wailing Wall. She's a bartender at Caesars Palace, and when the grief wave hit, she ran to the nearest women's restroom, hit the inner wall, and just sobbed. She told me how a woman who watched her said, "Oh honey, I feel your pain. I feel your pain." It made her laugh at the time, but it's true. Others *can* feel your pain. It holds so much energy. Everyone should find their own Wailing Wall as a safe place to grieve. Mine was a bathroom at work. Others may hear, but you can't stop the sounds any more than you could stop a train. It just is. Men most especially need a Wailing Wall because they think they need to be stoic and noble. No, they need a place to cry, sob, and scream as well. Crying every day for six months is very normal. It will taper off in its own time.

4. **See if there are some recent pictures, or maybe a recent video, that you can make still pictures from.** Put some you really like in beautiful frames and keep them in places where you often sit so you can see them frequently or make it a display on your cell phone or computer screen saver.

5. **Make a thin scrapbook and put in favorite pictures from your loved one's life.** Add their driver's license,

birth and death certificates. Add a meaningful trinket if it's appropriate—a medal, necklace, and so on. Make it a little memorial book that you can look at from time to time to remember the good times. When you look at it, you will feel poignant, sad, bittersweet, and very glad to have it because, most important, you will feel their love.

My daughter Nichole calls it torturing herself because it feels good when she listens to her husband Russ's favorite CDs even though she's crying while she's listening to them.

6. **You don't have to be in a hurry to get rid of the remains if your loved one was cremated.** Take all the time you need, and if you decide later that you want to keep them, you can have them put into a beautiful, sealed urn. My friend's husband told her to take a little of the ashes from his heart to keep, so she has a tiny heart shaped urn with some of his ashes that she keeps on her piano. It brings her comfort to see it there. She also had the urn in her closet for over a year and would open the closet door and tell him, "Hi Honey, I'm home." Only you know your loved one's remains are close to you.

7. **You don't have to be in a hurry to do something about your loved one's things.** It doesn't have to be all-or-nothing. I mentioned this to someone who told me her aunt's husband died. She was telling her aunt that it was time to let go of his things as nothing had been changed in the house. All his items were still around her. I asked her how old her aunt was. She said her aunt was seventy-four. My reply was, "Who cares if she keeps it the way it is? If it brings her comfort, she should keep it the way she wants." If it comforts people to keep shrines to their loved ones or not disturb a room, why should they do anything about it?

It isn't morbid. If it can bring comfort to sit in a room filled with your loved one's things, how can that possibly be wrong? We seem to want to judge. Who put us in charge?

When or if it feels the time is right to let go of some things, you can get a small trunk and put some favorite clothes, objects, toys, or whatever into the trunk and keep it in a closet. It's extremely comforting to know it's there even if you never look at it, and as time goes by (by this I mean *years*), you can let go bit by bit of things in the trunk until one day you may let go of the trunk entirely— or not—or put it in a smaller box or container. It's really up to you. Or maybe you will just have a bag left of special items as I do.

8. **Write in a journal**. Your thoughts and feelings are so damaged right now that the best place for them is on a piece of paper. Purge yourself. You can allow your anguish, guilt, and anger to spill out on a piece of paper. Writing can absorb some of your grief and give you an outlet of expression without worrying about hurting anyone's feelings. You can also write to your loved one who has passed. Write down the things you may not have said but wanted to say. Write about any guilt or anger you feel. Or just talk to your loved one on paper expressing your feelings as days go by. Who knows? Perhaps your loved is reading it over your shoulder?

9. **Forgiveness is another big issue**. Forgive yourself. The act of forgiving heals the forgiver. Forgiving another isn't for the person you're forgiving—it's for you. Forgiveness is the only way for you to truly heal. Think about the Lord's Prayer: "Forgive us our trespasses as we forgive our trespassers." There is a Guilt Release Hypnosis download on my website, lenayrogus.com, that is free for anyone who wants it. Realize that just about everyone feels guilt. A big one is that even though you were constantly at the side of

your loved one, just after you left to go to the bathroom, get a bite to eat, get some rest, and so on, your loved one passed away. So you weren't with him or her. Well, your loved one was probably waiting for you to leave so he or she could go without upsetting you. Guilt, guilt, guilt! We want to hang onto it. If we can't hang on to our loved ones, we can at least hang on to our guilt or anger. I can't emphasize enough how almost everyone who was in the classes I co-facilitated at the San Diego Hospice experienced some sort of guilt. Your healing depends upon your ability to let go of guilt. Your loved one's love for you is now unconditional. He or she doesn't want you to suffer.

10. **It is okay to be loud and noisy when you grieve.** You may have seen those photos of Jackie Kennedy looking quietly composed and stoic at President Kennedy's funeral, and how everyone commented on how "poised" she was. Of course, none of us saw her ranting and raving in her private grief. Can you really imagine going from living in the White House to who knows where? Going from the pinnacle of power to none? Oh, I think she was very angry for many reasons. It's almost as though society feels we should be quiet and not draw attention to ourselves, be noble and composed. When your child dies, you are NOT going to stand there quietly composed. You are probably going to yell, scream, sob, and maybe collapse and make a complete spectacle of yourself. So what? Do you really care what someone else thinks when you are going through such agony? I love how people in the Middle East make those high, shrill, undulating, warbling sounds. You know the ones I mean. We've all seen so much death in the Middle East on TV lately. It may be necessary to your sanity to be loud and let your grief out. Guided imagery can also help relieve stress, and I've included two examples on the following pages.

Up, Up, and Away— Balloon Relaxation Guided Imagery

My daughter has always loved this guided imagery. I hope you will, too.

Read it carefully and allow yourself to remember these easy relaxation steps. Or, if you would like a deeper relaxation, have someone read this to you or record it on your cell phone and listen to it later. Speak soothingly.

- *Get into a comfortable position lying down or sitting in a chair.*

- *Uncross your legs.*

- *Take off your glasses if you are wearing them.*

   Allow your eyes to close as you take a nice, easy breath through your nose and let it out slowly through your mouth. Take a second, deep breath and slowly let it out. Then take a third, deep, easy breath, and as you let it out, feel the tension loosen around your neck, your shoulders; your arms become limp and relaxed down even to your fingers. Pretend to feel a warm wave of comfort flowing from your head down to your toes.
   Deepen the relaxation by counting down from 3 to 1. When you reach 1, you will find yourself in a comfortable state of deeper relaxation.

- *3—deeper and deeper relaxed*

- *2—so comfortable and peaceful*

- *And 1—deeply relaxed*

Now, picture or imagine that you have a balloon tied to each wrist with a golden silk ribbon. You might notice that your arms are feeling lighter. And now also pretend that you have a balloon tied to each leg and around your waist. Notice what color your balloons are. These are your very own magical peace balloons so they can be any texture, color, or size you want. You might even have them all different colors, and notice if the balloons are smooth or bumpy or even covered with fabric or something else.

These balloons are now ready to take you on a wonderful, peaceful journey as you feel yourself getting lighter and lighter. There is nothing to do, nowhere else to be but right here in a peaceful place. Allow yourself to feel comfortably supported, almost as though you are riding on a cloud, as you find that your essence is expanding. It's even bigger than the room you are in, and now you are bigger than your home or apartment...and now you are bigger than your city...and your state. It's like looking down at a map as you look at everything from a different angle.

And now you are bigger than your country...and a sense of joy and wonder comes over you as you see yourself in space and looking down at the beautiful planet, Earth. You feel so free, so light in this magical space. For a moment, you've left the denseness of your body and allowed it to become light, almost transparent, and in this space you may sense a guardian or angel. If so, allow yourself to be aware of any message that may come to you. You feel a sense of direction and follow it to a beautiful crystal castle. The doors open and you are welcomed with love and open arms. You see the spirit of love waiting to comfort you as you relax in loving arms feeling protected, safe, and loved. This is a place of reverence and peace.

Just allow yourself to feel the bliss in this moment. It is a time of healing for your spirit, mind, and body, and now when you are ready, give thanks for this wonderful time and allow yourself to be back in the room, in the present, feeling calm and peaceful. And when you are ready, open your eyes, keeping that feeling of relaxation and healing with you.

My husband says this gentle relaxation process is like having a comfortable blanket over you.

Through the Window of Healing Guided Imagery

This is a process where you can talk to your loved one and say what you need to say and have your loved one respond so you get to hear what you need to hear. For those who are having an issue with guilt, please see my website, lenayrogus.com. There is a Guilt Release Hypnosis download that is free to all.

Because the goal of guided imagery or hypnosis is to take you on a journey, don't drive or operate machinery because you will be distracted.

Before listening to guided imagery, it is always good to make yourself very comfortable, lying down or sitting in a comfortable chair with your head supported. Uncross your legs and take off your glasses if you are wearing them.

As I ask you to breathe deeply—it calms and relaxes you to begin the process—also allow your eyes to close.

So, take a nice deep breath in through your nose and slowly let it out.

Again, one more deep breath in and sloooowly let it out.

And finally, a third deep breath in and gently let it out.

Close your eyes.

Good.

Now imagine or pretend that you are walking on a path in a beautiful green meadow. The path can be paved or dirt or even metal. Notice how your feet feel on this path. Are you barefoot? Is the path warm or rough? Is it cold or warm outside? You may feel a gentle breeze flow against your skin. Perhaps there is a tang in the air of pine trees or salty ocean air. The air smells clean and fresh, and you may even hear the whisper of leaves or the chatter of birds as you continue to walk until you notice a small clearing surrounded by trees, and in the middle of it is a comfortable rattan chair. You take a seat in the chair, surrounded by a magical area of peace. And in this special place of comfort, you notice a framed window hanging in the air. This is your "window of opportunity." This is your opportunity to hear what you need to hear and say what you need to say.

Allow the window to be filled by your loved one who has passed. You sense an acknowledgment between you. Maybe it's a smile or nod.

Now, tell your loved one what you need to tell him or her that you didn't get to say before. Let out all of the love, fear, anger, or guilt. Talk to your loved one and say what you need to say. Say everything. Good. (If you are recording this, give yourself time before you go on.)

Now, be your loved one. The subconscious mind cannot tell the difference between what is real and what is imagined, so become that person and tell yourself what you need to hear. Take your time. Make it real.

Now be yourself again and talk again, finding resolution and peace.

And now, be the one who has passed and tell yourself what you need to hear to bring you peace.

After all is said, thank your loved one and allow him or her and the window to magically vanish. Then get up from that chair in that magical place and start walking back down the path as you feel yourself becoming present in mind, body, and spirit again. You're back in the present but feeling better and more peaceful and calm.

And when you are ready, open your eyes, keeping that warm feeling as long as you can.

Chapter 6

The Degrees of Grief

People may be surprised that their grief is not as great as they expected, or it might be much worse. There are different types of grief, and sometimes you may not feel heavy grief when you expect to.

There is *inconsolable grief* that usually occurs when there is a sudden death, murder, suicide, accident, or loss of a child. There can also be inconsolable grief with the loss of a spouse or significant other, or even as a result of a sudden separation or divorce.

The death of a pet can also be very hard. Laurie, a dear friend of mine, was with her dog, Stella, when she was put to sleep. Laurie held Stella and tried to calm down her trembling. She felt that Stella knew she was dying. For Laurie, Stella was her child, and her grief was very strong. She told me her other dog would just look up and stare at an empty place, perhaps knowing Stella was visiting. My hairstylist told me her mother's dog had died, and her mother felt that the dog was like her granddaughter. Her mother was inconsolable in her grief.

Often, the degree of grief is a result of how close you are to the person who died. For instance, the death of someone you haven't seen in a while but were very close to might make you very sad, but you will not be devastated. My wonderful mom had terminal cancer, and I felt grief every time I saw her. Upon her death I was terribly sad, but relieved that the suffering was finally over. I was grieving for a long time, watching her as she deteriorated bit by pain-filled bit, and then she finally died. I suffered right along with her. I was set free as well, even though that doesn't seem politically correct to say or even feel. But it's true. Yes, I grieved for a long while but also felt relieved that her suffering was finally over.

Sometimes, a parent may die whom you've been angry with for a long time. It may take years for those warmer feelings under the surface to rise to the top. Often, grief happens then. It can also be this way with an estranged sibling. And that's okay. It happens. Allow your feelings of bitterness and anger toward them to surface; get through them and come out the other side, finally letting go of them. I worked with a terminally ill woman who held tremendous anger toward her sister. Through guided imagery and discussion, she finally forgave her sister. I was glad that she felt at peace when she herself died.

And there is the very real grief a person feels who has mental illness, been in an accident, has had a body part amputated, or suffers from post traumatic stress disorder (PTSD). These cause enormous grief not only for the person suffering but also for their loved ones. Lives are changed forever. Our wounded warriors and their families go through so much. Divorce and sudden breakups can make you doubt yourself along with causing inconsolable grief. Even major career events like not passing the bar or being fired from a job can cause deep depression and self-doubt.

I can't imagine the grief involved in surviving a major flood, fire, or tornado. You lose everything: your home, your job, and your belongings.

Many people are told that grief comes in stages, from anger through acceptance. There is also the belief that grief begins with strong feelings that become less and less over time. I didn't find either to be true, other than okay, well, give me enough years and it does become less, until something jars me back into feeling grief all over again. Sometimes, I think grief is just two tablespoons deep. I'm fine, but if I allow myself to really go back and think about the actual time of death, I'll start to cry again. It's true that I can usually get over it quickly, but I'm talking twenty years or more later.

Anger can be felt at various times during the grieving process. I know I got very angry at Jack. I didn't know how to program our advanced stereo system because I had relied on him to do it, so I sat on the floor and pounded it as I cried in anger and grief. And you should have seen me with the power drill. Instead of a drill bit, I put in a wrench key (which is square and dull) and didn't understand why I couldn't make a hole. Sometimes, the anger is all you can hold onto. If the courts are involved, the grief again has a direction.

Many of us feel we must do something to give our lives meaning after a terrible loss, especially from a sudden death or crime. Often good comes from this need to do something worthwhile. Mothers Against Drunk Driving (MADD) was started from this premise as was John Walsh's TV program, *America's Most Wanted*. The Three-Day Walk for Breast Cancer and the amazing fund-raising work done for AIDS research happened because of the grief of so many who came together for a cause. That is the gift from grief.

Your grief can be very strong in the beginning, and after a while you may feel you are getting better, then another day your grief is just as great as it was the first day. This is what makes the journey so difficult. How long does it take to get over your grief? There is no time table for it or rationale about it. You may feel normal again and laugh and enjoy life, but the grief is there within a few moments of contemplation. Depending upon the severity of your grief, it can take many years to overcome. But no matter what you do, the empty place in your heart stays with you all of your life. You just adapt to it. You can and will be happy again. Just believe that.

Part II
The Journey Begins

Chapter 7

My First Loss

I was just a little girl, only seven years old, when I started this journey. I loved to sing and dance and to look in the mirror and talk to it. I was a bit aggressive if I didn't get my way. In first grade, I ran a race with some kids and another girl won by a few steps. I was not nice. I pulled her hair and started a fight that ended in the principal's office. But by seven, I had toned it down a bit and had friends in the neighborhood. My mom, stepdad, and sisters worked during the day, and my grandmother, Baba, would look after me.

On one day that changed my life, my Baba was visiting her son in another state, and I was left alone. It didn't really bother me because I played with my friends and didn't think about it.

My friend Sharon came over to play, and we noticed there was a large, burned-out tree trunk lying on the ground right outside our porch. It must have been put there by our neighbor until it could be taken away. You know how Shakespeare said, "All the world's a stage"? Well in looking back, it did seem the scene was set, and we walked right into it.

"How fun, let's play operator." I'm sure I said something like that. My sister Millie was a telephone operator, and this particular tree was on the ground with a large broken branch sticking up at the top of it. The branch was about a foot wide, and at the base was a hole about two inches in diameter. And lying right next to the trunk was a group of wires tied together just the right size to fit in that hole. The wide branch also had a lot of holes in it, so we could play operator. I went first and straddled the trunk and put the wires in the hole at the base. They fit perfectly. So I started putting wires in the holes and pretending to talk to people.

One of the wires sprung out and hit me in the nose, so I put it back in the same hole. It sprung out again, but this time it hit me right in the center of my eye and sprung out again. I screamed because it was so painful, and then started to cry and couldn't stop. Sharon got scared and said she was going home. I begged her to stay with me, but when she wouldn't, I made her promise not to tell anyone.

I was still crying from the pain as I went into the house, and I ran to the bathroom sink and threw handfuls of water in my eye. Finally, the pain started to subside a bit, and I went into my mother's bedroom and looked in the mirror. I closed one eye to look out the injured one, and it was streaking down, all the colors melting together, as though a paintbrush stroked down a canvas. I was trembling, scared, and in pain, so I lay down on top of my mom's satin bedspread and covered myself with it and cried myself to sleep.

When Mom came home, she woke me up and looked at me. She asked me what had happened. I was so afraid that I couldn't tell her. I thought they might take my eye. I just said I didn't feel good. I'd recently had measles, and Mom thought I had measles on my eye. In those days, people didn't run to the local Urgent Care if they were ill. They just dealt with it. I don't remember much about what happened after the event, but any time taking me to the doctor was mentioned, I ran out the back door and hid outside for hours before coming back in.

And then the headaches started. Agonizing headaches that made me writhe in my bed. My Baba would pray over me and rub my forehead with lemons, but nothing would help. I don't remember how long that lasted, but my vision in my right eye slowly went to gray. I could still see some movement, but then it went dark.

Mom suspected something was wrong, and she would make me take a pack of cigarettes and put them over my good eye and ask me how many fingers she was holding up. I was very good at peeking and always gave the right answer. But I became very clumsy, and the family took to calling me "doppey." I couldn't hold a cup of liquid straight in my right hand. And I inadvertently walked into things.

As time went on, my personality changed. I went from being outgoing and exuberant to introverted and painfully shy. My teachers complained that my writing was only one-eighth of an inch high and wanted my family to get me to write in larger letters.

As the years went by, we moved around a lot, so I went to different schools and never made many friends. Books became my friends. I was a good student, but mostly a loner. By this time, I had a large scar over my right pupil that almost covered the iris. My eye was also starting to wander until I became wall-eyed. I felt disfigured. Kids were uncomfortable around me.

When I was eleven and in sixth grade, my teacher told us she was giving us all an eye exam. She put an eye chart on the blackboard and had students come up one by one to take the test. Then it was my turn. I was so scared when she called me. My face was red and my heart was racing. I had never revealed my secret to anyone in four years. The paddle to hold over each eye was large, so I couldn't peek around it. I took the test with my left eye first, but then I had to put the paddle over the left eye and look with my right.

I told the teacher, "I don't see the letters."

She said, "Well, just walk farther away until you can."

I walked halfway up the aisle and said again, "I don't see the letters."

Then she said, "Well, walk forward until you can."

I felt so vulnerable and embarrassed with everyone looking at me. I was choked up with that pain in my throat as I held back my tears and walked slowly straight up to the board with my nose almost touching it, and I said, "I can't see them."

I felt so humiliated and sad. The teacher just called the next student.

I guess the school must have called my mom because very soon after that, she had one of her customers take me to an optometrist to get my eyes checked out. She didn't have a car and felt her friend would look after me. I finally told the doctor the truth after he examined me. After all, he could see there was a major problem. I told him the whole story, and he just shook his head and told me how lucky I was that I didn't get an infection.

After that, Mom took me herself to a top ophthalmologist who had worked wonders for soldiers in World War II. He did a lot of tests and finally told us there was nothing he could do about the vision, but when I was fully grown at sixteen, he could straighten my eyes and remove most of the scar tissue. But I had to wait five more years.

During those years, we moved many times, and I went to a number of schools, so by the beginning of my junior year in high school, I was starting at a new school. I met with a counselor who I remember to this day with such gratitude. He realized how terribly shy I was and told me I should take an acting class. I was terrified, but he gave me a note to give to the teacher. So I walked to the theater, opened the big metal doors that clanged shut behind me as I walked across the wooden stage, my footsteps echoing, and went to the other wing of the stage where the class was. The students were on each side of a middle aisle, and the teacher was at the far end. I sucked in my breath and walked forward to hand the note to the teacher. He looked at it and said he didn't have any more room in the class. He wrote something on the note and told me to take it back to the counselor, Mr. LaFerla. So I did.

This wonderful counselor looked at the note, shook his head and said, "Oh, no," wrote back on the note, and told me to take it back to the teacher. Now I'm shy, right…really, really shy. It took so much courage for me to march back through those big metal doors, again slamming behind me, taking that lonely, loud walk back across the stage, facing those students again as I quickly walked up to the teacher and handed him the note once more. He read it and calmly pointed to a chair in the front row and said, "Take a seat." I don't remember more of that day, but Ken Ton became my favorite teacher. I took theater that year, did summer stock theater, took it my senior year, and I was able to participate in the summer theater group after I graduated.

Acting gave me the opportunity to slip into a different character and become a new person. I could put on the character and become it. It was wonderful—liberating. I started to come out of my shell and shine a little bit. That summer I was sixteen, and Mom pulled in every favor possible to get me the eye surgery. I started school again as a senior with both eyes straight and a tiny scar that most people could never see. I blossomed and became popular, but I was always haunted and traumatized by the injury. I could never talk about it without crying. I was in my early thirties before I finally made peace with the situation. Almost all the time, I forget that I'm not seeing out of my right eye. I do tell people who work with me that if they want to get my attention, they need to make a noise; otherwise, it will seem as though I'm ignoring them. But it no longer bothers me.

In retrospect, this whole episode in my life built my character. I'm much more compassionate with others, and I see all viewpoints without becoming judgmental. I accept and like myself.

I will continue to share my journey by telling you about my family in detail in the next several chapters. I want to bring them to life for you by telling their stories so you can see them as I do and know how losing them affected me, and how I came through my loss and grief and healed. Hopefully, something that you read will be of help to you in your grief and will give you comfort that you, too will heal.

Chapter 8

Baba, Earth Mother

My grandmother, Sophia, was a very strong woman. So was my mother. I think I came from a long line of strong women who lived hard lives. I called my grandmother "Baba", which means grandmother in Serbian. She was born in Yugoslavia (which is now Serbia) in a town that doesn't exist anymore. It was wiped out by the Germans in World War I. My Grandfather Daniel and my mom's older brother, Bronco, came to America before World War I, and Baba was left with my mom and my mom's brother Leo, who was two years older than her: Mom was three and Leo five. It was usual during that time for men to go to America, get a job, get settled, and then send for their families.

During the war, Mom told me that Baba would hide her and Leo in the incinerator out back when the German soldiers came to the house. I never thought about it until I was older, but Baba was in her thirties, alone except for two small children, and who knows what the soldiers demanded of her. Eventually, her house was burned down, but I remember seeing a photo she saved of the family. It was burned around the edges.

Baba told me that all the remaining men and women in the town were given shovels and made to dig their own graves. As they were ready to be shot and killed, the American army stopped the slaughter and rescued them. I've heard that many towns were eradicated by the Germans during World Wars I and II.

In 1921, Baba, Mom, and Leo came to America. Mom was ten. While Baba was pretty severe in her treatment of Mom, she doted on her two boys, Leo and Bruno, even though Bruno was much older. They owned a boarding house, and my grandpa worked in the mines; he suffered an injury in a mining accident that left him blind. I remember guiding him around the house and up and down the stairs; he called me his eyes. He died when I was three, and I still have a memory of a vision of seeing four angels, each taking a corner of his casket and ascending with it.

Long before I was born, when Mom was thirteen, she wanted a pair of silk stockings. Mom was a hard worker at the boarding house. She cleaned rooms and washed clothes for the boarders, and she also attended school. At thirteen, she rebelled. Baba told her if she wanted silk stockings, she had to go out and make money on her own to buy them.

My Uncle Bronco was more than ten years older than my mom. He was a bootlegger and was familiar with the speakeasies. As young as he was, he may have either owned one or ran one. He could be brutal, but he definitely would have looked out for my mom. At thirteen, Mom quit school, put on some very high heels, and started working as a cocktail waitress in the speakeasy. She was very buxom and looked much older.

My great, great grandmother was a gypsy who married a Serbian orthodox priest. It was okay for them to marry. I sometimes wonder if there is a psychic gene in my family because my grandmother could read cards, as did her mother and mother before her, and on down the line to me. We moved so often during my school years. Mom would just say it was the gypsy in her soul that made her wander. I think it was the bookies.

We had our home in the back of a beauty shop in Ohio where I was born, and Baba would read cards for Mom's best customers. She never took any money. She called it a gift from God. But she would accept bakery goods or food in return. I remember whenever we had to toss away bread because it had grown moldy, Baba would kiss the bread and say a quick prayer. In thinking about it now, I realize she must have experienced hunger many times in her life.

I remember my Baba as both a strict disciplinarian but also a kind woman. She would have me go out and get a switch from a tree branch when I behaved badly. She also pulled my hair, hard, which I *hated*. But I also remember how she would go through the toilet and look at my bowel movement when I was afraid I might have worms. She would even take it in her hand and sift through it to reassure me that nothing was there. I was very young to have this phobia, but I did. I would hold my bowels in until I couldn't any more, then cry, and run to Baba until she told me everything was all right.

I think this phobia started when I heard that my mom had a tapeworm when she came over from Europe. I was one of those children who thought I had every illness that I heard about.

In the evenings, Baba would sit at the dining table, which was covered in a lace tablecloth, with three lit candles in front of her. She would play with a piece of thread between her thumb and forefinger and pray…and pray…and pray for what seemed to be an hour. That's an awfully long time for a child to sit and watch and not speak. Not that I was supposed to be there, but sometimes I would watch her pray and squirm around in my seat and try to put my fingers through the holes in the lace. She would bless dimes that she put in our shoes for protection. Nothing bothered her. After she was done, she would pour a shot of whiskey and down it. It wasn't until I was a grown woman that I realized she was actually meditating. My grandmother was a very spiritual person. I'm certain that her spiritual belief is what got her through the bad times. She would always say, "God will provide." Well, she was rescued from digging her own grave, so no wonder she believed this.

She also played with me. She taught me Serbian words while I sat on her lap and pointed to this and that. And she baked the most wonderful cakes and cookies. She mixed up her Serbian and English words. My sister Millie loved to go bowling, and Baba would say "Millie pushta de balla."

When I was eight, Baba fell and broke her hip, and after that she used a walker. It looked like a box with a seat at one end, not the small ones we see today. The seat lifted up so she could step into it. She could get very close to the stove, stand, move to it, and still cook. Nothing seemed to slow her down until the arthritis in her knees did.

Baba moved in with my sister Betty who was eleven years older than me. Betty had two children, Vicki and Steve, and Baba looked after the kids, made meals, and let them hang and play on her walker.

When my Niece Vicki was born, I was only seven. I loved her so much, and Baba would let me take her to the front porch where I would sit with her and hold her. Sometimes, I held her so close that I would make her cry just so I could soothe her. When I got tired of her, I'd open the front door and let her crawl in. I'm sure Baba was looking out for her. Hey, I was only seven. I had things to do outside, like go play.

My grandmother had advanced arthritis in her knees that brought her a great deal of pain, and at seventy-five, she was admitted to the hospital with arteriosclerosis. I remember seeing her there, and she seemed happy and alert. I had no idea it was fatal. It was the last time I saw her.

When I was fourteen, Mom told me Baba had died. I was devastated. It was my first experience with death. My grandmother was a very strong woman, as was my mother, as I am, and so is my daughter. Perhaps grief forges us to be more than we would be otherwise.

I don't remember much of my grandmother's funeral. I know I was there, but I just don't remember that day in detail. It is so interesting how the mind blocks out what we don't want to remember. I know I cried a great deal and was at the burial site. My only regret is that I didn't have the time to really know her or ask her in detail about her life. Her life was so rich with experience. It really is too bad that we don't question our elders about their lives in detail. Their histories are so full, but they go with them when they leave us.

I suggest you ask your elders about their lives and to tell you their stories. It will be a gift to you when they are gone.

Chapter 9

Momma, Independent before Her Time

My mom was my everything, both father and mother. When I was sixteen, I remember sitting in a chair in a booth in a beauty shop where she was working as she did my hair. My heart filled up with so much love for her that I could barely talk. I couldn't even get the words, "Mom, I love you," out of my mouth. I just sat there with a lump in my throat as my eyes filled up with tears.

People would call her an angel, but to me she was my inspiration. She always told me to look up. If I smiled, the world would smile with me. She didn't laugh when I told her I wanted to be an actress; she just told me I could be whatever I wanted. She was my rock.

My mom came to America when she was ten years old. She had a beautiful Serbian name, but there were too many *j*'s and *c*'s in it to pronounce correctly, so they named her Elsie Helen when she went through Ellis Island. I understand now that both Serbia and Slovakia are separate countries after the breakup of Yugoslavia. My family would say that we were Serbian and Slovakian, so I guess we're both.

Mom was teased mercilessly by the other children when she went to school. She tried so hard to pronounce English words correctly. She was so embarrassed that she was determined to conquer not only the English language but correct pronunciation as well. She eliminated all traces of any accent. Think about the Russian and Slavic people you hear now; most of them have an accent. Think Zsa Zsa Gabor and her sisters. My mom was determined to sound like any other American. I've been told that it is easier to lose an accent when you are young.

I mentioned before that she started working at a speakeasy

when she was thirteen. Well, she was well before her time as an emancipated woman. She was a tireless worker and had great determination. As so often happened during that time, when she was eighteen, Mom entered into an arranged marriage. She moved to a large ranch in Maryland with her husband and his parents. There, she was treated more like an indentured servant than a family member. She took care of the farmhands and the family and she had my sister, Millie. She also endured beatings from her husband.

As I said, we sort of have a psychic gene in my family. Mom said that she woke up suddenly one night and saw a light shoot across her vision, and she knew that her mother-in-law had died. She woke her husband up, and they found out it was so.

Two years after Millie was born, Momma was pregnant with Betty. She still had to work just as hard as before, but one night her father-in-law said, "Elsie, what would you do without us?" Well, Mom decided to find out what it would be like to be free of her servitude. After all the verbal abuse and the beatings, she packed her bags, took Millie, and walked out the door. Her husband— she called him "Fats"—didn't like that very much. So, according to Mom, he came after her in his car and tried to run her down. Unfortunately, I never did get the complete story of how she escaped. My cousin told me later that she climbed a hill and a bus came to a stop just as she reached the top. She got on the bus and was out of harm's way. She went back home to Ohio and divorced Fats Martz. He never tried to get in touch with her or his children. Maybe that was a good thing.

Before the Great Depression hit, Mom was determined to go to beauty school so she could earn good money, especially for a woman at that time. She was creative and loved working with hair. After she was graduated, the Depression hit big time. But women who had extreme wealth kept their fortune, as we see with what has happened to us recently. So Mom took advantage of the fact that women always wanted to look beautiful. She would take a bus to a wealthy woman's home, do her hair, and take the bus back home. When she dated, she would always say she would cook if her date brought the food. Smart lady! She always had food in the house when so many were going hungry.

A few years later in the late thirties, she met Nick Penovich. He was in love with her, but she was looking for security not only for her children but also for her mother and father. She didn't love Nick, but she entered into a marriage plus a business arrangement with him. He felt he loved her enough for both of them. He bought a two-story house, and much of the first story was turned into a beauty shop. This was the first shop she owned, and she was good at what she did.

Mom decided she wanted to learn how to drive. So one day early on, she was driving by herself when her car stalled and died. She couldn't get it restarted, and she was in the middle of traffic. A man in the car behind her leaned on the horn for a long time. So Mom got out of the car, went to the man, and told him, "I'll kindly lean on that horn if you'll fix my car." But the incident shook her up, and she never drove again.

Like any good business owner, Mom attended civic events and community meetings that were much like today's networking groups. One day, she met a man named Jim McCullough who was the campaign manager for John McSweeney in Ohio who was running for the senate in 1940 and Mom fell in love for the first time in her life at thirty-one years old. World War II had started, and from what I was told, once the war started, Jim McCullough did intelligence work here after Pearl Harbor was bombed.

They had a torrid love affair for a few years, and I was the result. I was born Marie Kay Penovich, but my family called me "Cookie" because the comics had a *Blondie and Dagwood* strip, and they had just brought home their daughter, Cookie. Jim would see her as often as he could, and she would meet him at various places. Nick thought I was his at first, and his family always did. So did I. But it was an open secret in my family. Both of my sisters and Mom's niece knew. I'm sure Baba knew. They had all met him. Jim knew me. Mom would take me to see him every time they could get together, and he loved me from what I was told.

Now here is where it gets interesting. Mom said she took me to California to see Jim. He was flying into California, and she wanted to be there because the war was over and they wanted to start a life together. Mom said he died in a plane crash. My cousin told me another story, however. She said that Jim wanted Mom and me to be with him but not my teenage sisters and grandparents. While Mom was in California with me, her father died. Mom was grandpa's favorite, and she took it very hard.

In any event, when I was three years old, Mom left Nick Penovich. We all moved to California and lived in Pasadena. I loved Nick and thought my Daddy didn't want me. I felt abandoned by him. Shortly thereafter, Mom purchased another beauty shop, and we lived in the back of it. My sister Betty loved Nick, too, because he was the only father she ever knew. This sense of abandonment stayed with me most of my life. I always would get tongue-tied around authority figures and feel intimidated. That was a pretty difficult burden to carry around considering that most of my life was spent as an executive secretary surrounded by people of authority and power. I faked it, though and presented a very professional façade.

I didn't find out that Jim was my real father until I was twenty-one, when I asked Mom if he was because she would always talk about him as if he were the sun and the moon. She was never bitter toward him and always would say how he had inspired her. Since she felt that way, I'm more inclined to believe her story rather than my cousin's. But I still don't know what really happened to him or between them.

After Mom had her beauty shop for a while, she discovered her love of the "nags," as she called them. She absolutely loved the horse races and would study her racing forms and figure the odds. She was fond of saying this was her only vice. But it was a *big* one. She was a gambler pure and simple, and the bookies were both her friends and her enemies. She probably would have become wealthy except for her "little" vice. I was taken to every racetrack in Southern California and Tijuana before I was six. I still don't enjoy them.

When I was five years old, I was riding my tricycle in front of the beauty shop that faced Vermont Avenue in Los Angeles. This is a main street with tons of traffic. I must have gotten too close to the curb, and the tricycle and I fell headlong into oncoming traffic. I hit my chin on either the bike or the curb, split it open, and lost consciousness. My sister Millie ran out of the shop and rescued me. I don't remember any of it except in the dreams I've had all my life where I'm lying down in the street and rolling around feeling I cannot get up and trying to avoid the cars coming at me.

Not too long after that, I was playing in our little backyard that had an alley running through it. My sister Betty was going out with a Marine named Marty Martin. The back door was open with just the screen across it. I remember a large man with a butcher knife standing in front of me and mesmerizing me like a cobra. He said, "I'm going to kill you." Just as he said that, Marty dived through the screen door and tackled him. I remember that incident but nothing after that. It's like a snapshot in my head of pure terror. I'm sure he was turned over to the police. Not long after that, Mom sold the shop to a gunsmith and we moved away.

By the way, she never would let me have a bike after that accident. I'm probably the only person I know who doesn't know how to ride a bike.

Mom married again when I was seven to a wonderful man named Edwin McKinney. We all called him Pappy or Mac. I called him Daddy. I remember one day as he was scrubbing the floor, I ran across the hallway and said, "Hi, Daddy." He was so cool. I remember he smiled to himself and kept scrubbing the floor. It was so hard for me to say that, and he so loved my saying it. I loved him with all of my heart.

We all lived in Lawndale, California, in a small, rented house. Baba, my two sisters Millie and Betty, and I all slept in a large dining room. Mom and Mac had the bedroom. My grandmother looked after me while Mom went to work.

The little boy across the street came down with polio and had to go into an iron lung. He was my friend, so I saw him all the time. Around that time, I started having terrible pains in my legs. Mom said it was growing pains. Nevertheless, Pappy would spend a long time every night massaging and maneuvering my legs while

I cried from the pain. This went on for a long time. Was it related to polio? I'll never know. Pappy also cuddled me all the time after I injured myself.

When I was eleven, I was in the house when Millie and Pappy got into an argument. Pappy accused her of arranging for Mom to meet a man, and my sister just taunted him as was her way. Millie was twenty-four at the time and had recently come to live with us. Pappy got so angry that he started strangling her. Mom came out of the kitchen with a large knife, and I ran out the door and hid in the garage behind the washer and shook. I was terrified.

After about an hour, I got my courage together and walked back into the house, not knowing what to expect. Everyone was acting normally, and no one said anything about what had happened. It was surreal. But the next day when I came home from school, Pappy had moved out. I never saw him again, and I was devastated. I grieved and was so sad. I felt abandoned again.

At this point, my mom started gambling pretty heavily, and we moved around a lot. Sometimes, the places were nice homes; other times, they were old, dingy places, and one time we were in a very tiny trailer for a few months. I moved twenty times during my school years. A lot of times we moved around and I stayed at the same school. Other times, I had to change schools, too. As Mom would say, it was just the gypsy in her soul, but I knew she couldn't always pay back her bookies. Sometimes, she was threatened, but in the end, she would get the money somehow.

Mom started up another beauty shop for one of her customers when I was around fifteen. She was supposed to get a percentage, but nothing was in writing. Mom continued to work there for a long time.

My sister Betty really encouraged me to learn how to type and take dictation to become a secretary. She said that I had to learn how to be independent and make good money because no one else could do it for me. She told me to never rely on another person to take care of me. Those were the days when men and women married early, and often the woman stayed at home and didn't work at all. That was the best advice I ever got.

After I was graduated from high school, I immediately got a civil service job as a secretary working for the Air Force Ballistic Missile Division. I also went to a junior college and took classes in music composition, voice, and theater, along with advanced shorthand and English composition. I wanted to be an actress, but through luck, started working for Universal Studios in their secretarial pool. When I say through luck, it really was. There was a very nice man who I would talk to at the commissary at lunch. He was a cameraman. One day, he asked me why I wasn't doing something more interesting like working for the motion picture industry. I laughed and thought it was some type of come on. But he persisted and convinced me that he would set up an interview for me at Universal Studios. He kept his word, despite my disbelief, and I met with the head of the steno pool who hired me on the spot. Life can be so unpredictable.

Those days at Universal were so interesting. A lot of major stars worked in the bungalows. This was before the large black tower of offices there now. We would see Rock Hudson and Cary Grant walking together to the commissary for lunch. I was working for a producer and a writer in a bungalow next to Cary Grant's and across from Alfred Hitchcock's. Lots of television shows were being produced on the lot, too. This was still the era when stars were under studio contract, not like now.

One day, I was walking down the path to my car, and for some reason, Cary Grant took an interest in me. His bungalow was next to where I was working, and he bounded through the grass to my side and said, "I say, you're rather shy, aren't you?" We talked for a while. He would stop me and talk to me from time to time on my way out of the office, and he showed me his office and introduced me to his secretary and producer. He was very kind and took me to dinner once.

I never tried to capitalize on my work or contacts in order to act; I never even mentioned it. But I never understood his interest. Once he walked up to me in the commissary as I was eating alone, and he put both of his hands on the table and leaned over to say, "Hello, Marie." Now everyone is looking at Cary Grant, right? Who wouldn't? He was gorgeous and a *big star*. I looked him straight in the eyes and said, "You know you're embarrassing me, right?" He just laughed and walked away.

One day, I was on the way to lunch at the commissary with some of my friends, and we saw Cary Grant and Rock Hudson walking together about twenty feet before us. The girls got all crazy and acted like big fans, but I was embarrassed and slowed down until they were ten feet in front of me. I noticed that two male extras saw these two big stars coming and held the doors open for them, then let the doors close right before the girls were entering. The girls mumbled angrily and opened the doors themselves and went in. By the time I reached the door, Cary Grant opened it for me and apologized for the men. What? Did he have eyes in the back of his head?

On another occasion, while walking out of my office after work, Cary was leaving his office at the same time and saw me and came over to me. He asked me if I would like to have dinner with him at his home. Well, I'm not stupid! Of course I said yes. He said he would lead me in his car and I should follow him home.

So what's it really like to go out with a number one box office, top-level movie star who is gorgeous and loved and adored by everyone? Well, it's surreal. I wasn't star struck because I worked with so many of them, but hello? I followed Cary in my car until we were at the bottom of a hill in Coldwater Canyon. He had stopped and waited for me and told me he would drive me up the hill to his home. So, there I was in the front seat of a Rolls Royce, and I couldn't help but run my hand over the soft gray, smooth calfskin seats. His home overlooked Beverly Hills, and I could see all the twinkling lights. It got dark early at that time of year, so I couldn't see the grounds around his house very well. We went into his home, and he introduced me to his housekeeper-cook.

Then he took me back to his bedroom where he did his entertaining. Walking through the house, I noticed that half of his furniture was covered in sheets because he was planning to leave for London where he also had a home. He told me he stayed half the year in England and half in America. He had a large, adjustable king-size bed, and we sat back and talked and watched TV. There was a movie on, and he told me how much he liked the actor in the lead.

I was only nineteen, and he was in his forties. I remember looking at him and thinking, "How can I be here with this lovely man who is bigger than life?" He was a perfect gentleman—no leering or propositions. Perhaps he was lonely and didn't want someone who was all starry-eyed but just appreciated being with him as I did. We were comfortable together and got along well. His housekeeper came in with dinner for us on individual trays.

Now, what would you think a "big star" would eat at home? Just what you might imagine. First, I was offered a champagne cocktail (my first ever) and toast triangles with caviar. I'd never had caviar, either, but I liked it. Then dinner was lamb chops with mint jelly and asparagus with Hollandaise sauce. After that, we were served a small vanilla ice cream sundae with a cookie.

We talked and watched the rest of the movie, then he drove me back down to my car, and I went home. He continued to talk to me every now and then before he went to England. I left Universal shortly after that and never saw him again. It's a wonderful memory, though.

Ironically, that same night I came home from his house and got out of the car, I was approached by a man who asked the time. I told him but thought it was odd because a big time-temperature clock could be seen from our street.

A while after I got into my apartment, there was a knock on the door. I opened it, and it was the same man. He wanted to know if there were any apartments for rent. I pointed to the manager's apartment and told him to go there to find out. He then asked if he could use the phone and walked in and picked up the receiver. I felt this strange sense of danger and leaned against the open door with my feet on the threshold. Then he came up behind me, put a knife to my neck, and said, "Don't scream or I'll kill you." So I screamed and screamed and screamed. He dropped the knife and ran as all my neighbors came out. I was shaking. Someone called the police, and we went looking for him but never found him. I was so naïve, so young. He must have waited to see which light came on in the window to see where I lived and then followed me. What a way to end a wonderful experience.

After that, I started having panic attacks, and my behavior changed probably because this was the third time I had been threatened at knifepoint, and my subconscious remembered. My performance on my job suffered as a result, and my supervisor fired me, never bothering to ask me if anything was wrong and not knowing what had happened. It took me six months under a doctor's care to get enough confidence back so I didn't run into the house after locking my car. But I did heal.

A year later, I was accepted into a theater group in Hollywood, the Three Arts Studio, and started doing musical comedies. We performed forty-eight shows at military bases, hospitals, prisons, and locally. I was part of the theater group for ten years and performed frequently.

During this time, Mom opened up another beauty shop in Orange County near Disneyland. There was a lot of stress, and it became just too much for her; she was all alone out there. She eventually moved back into Hawthorne where I went to school, and she lived with my sisters and Betty's children, my dear Niece Vivian, and Nephew Steve.

Mom had a heart attack when I turned twenty-one. From her hospital bed, she made Betty and Millie promise to take me out for a drink on my birthday. It was a pretty sad occasion. The good news was that Mom recovered, but she never worked again. My mom, who could work tirelessly, finally had to slow down at the age of 52.

When Mom came out of the hospital, she moved in with me, and we lived in Hollywood. I was working at Northrop Corporation in Beverly Hills, which is now Northrop Grumman, for the corporate advertising manager as his secretary. I had auditioned for a part in a play, and after the interview, the producer found out that I was an executive secretary and could take dictation, so he offered me a job working for him to help write his script for a new movie. He offered me a part in the movie and the opportunity to travel with him to Europe when the script was completed. He wanted to do a joint venture with a studio there. After a couple of months when the script was written, he kept his word, and I went with him to England, Germany, Austria, Hungary, Belgrade, and Bermuda. We were welcomed at the motion picture studios in most of those countries. What a wonderful opportunity this was for me, not only as an all-expense-paid visit to many of the capitols in Europe but I was also being paid to do it.

Unfortunately, the producer's wife wasn't happy about the trip and threatened to divorce him. So when we returned to California, I was out of a job. Yes, I was young, and I was naïve, but not dumb. We didn't have any type of personal encounter as his wife had imagined, but it was obvious she was unhappy about the trip even though she knew I would be traveling with him, and she had even paid my wages and deposited my salary into my bank. In retrospect, it felt as though I'd won the lottery, and it is a wonderful memory.

After a year, my girlfriend Micki moved in with us. Mom would make us breakfast in the morning as we barely had our eyes open. It was a fun, fun time. We did a lot of shows together. When I got married, Micki went on the road as a singer and comedienne with her male partner. My niece and Millie moved in with Mom and so did another of my girlfriends. But she also got married and moved out.

For some reason, probably because of my early childhood, Mom always felt that I needed to be protected and that I wasn't strong enough emotionally to endure hardship. But she was wrong. I was just as strong-willed and determined as she was, and as I endured each major life event that happened, I got even stronger.

I had been married for seven years and was pregnant with my second child when Mom asked me to take her to the doctor. We were told she had colon cancer and that it was incurable. It was devastating news to all of us. My mom was my rock, and it seemed unreal that I was going to lose her.

Mom had always been afraid to fly, but since she had "nothing to lose"—so she said—she flew to Hawaii where my sister Betty was living and stayed with her until she became too ill. Then she returned home.

Vicki took care of Mom while I was busy taking care of my husband, a new baby, and my two-year-old daughter. My last visit to Mom in the hospital was very difficult. She was miserable and rocking and moaning in pain. I told her that my son Chad got his first tooth. I talked to her and kissed her. As I was leaving, she gave me a small wave and said, "Good-bye." (Oh, was that hard to write.) She died that night. I still grieve for her, and it's been forty years since she died.

At the funeral, I saw her in a coffin, dressed beautifully as always, but she was dead. After that, I vowed never to look at anyone I loved after they were dead. That image always stays with you, and I wanted to remember the image of her alive.

I still dream about her. In one dream, we have a good time together, but she just doesn't want to give me her address. In another wonderful dream I had, I was in the "in-between" place and saw a lot of people sitting in chairs facing away from me as I was going down an aisle. A woman stood up and came toward me and gave me a fierce hug. I knew it was Momma even though she didn't look the same, and I felt such love. I woke up with that memory and feeling. I felt she had visited me.

I really do believe you can hug your loved one who has passed away. In that place just as you awaken in the morning, you can picture your loved one and see yourself giving her or him a big hug and feel it returned. For that instant, it can seem very real because the love is real and never goes away.

My mom was a very spiritual woman even though she didn't go to church. She held her belief in her heart, and it was strong. She was truly an inspirational woman, always looking for the best in people, and she expected to find it. People called her an angel while she was alive. What greater compliment can there be than that?

It took time for me to allow myself to grieve fully for Mom. When she died, Jack had recently returned from the hospital, and the babies were so small and needy that I put my feelings on hold. It was a difficult time for all of us in so many ways, but I knew my mom was in a better place…that she had gone Home.

I started grieving for my mom when we found out she was terminally ill. It took a year, but each time I saw her, I felt her slipping away from us. It's really hard to see how pain can cause the deterioration of body and spirit. It was so sad to see her fight that battle. It is very difficult to see our loved ones suffer and gradually get worse when we can do nothing to help. You cry, but don't want them to see you crying. And finally, when the pain is over for them and they have passed, you feel a sense of relief because they are no longer suffering, and yet you no longer have them in your life to love and encourage you, to kiss your troubles away. In some ways, I healed faster because I'd been grieving for over a year. But she knows I miss her to this day, and I feel that she watches over me.

Chapter 10

Jack, Courageous and Noble

A little seven-year-old boy was happily sauntering home from school and turned onto his street when he heard a boy call out, "Jack, your mom is dead." A curtain came down, and Jack Drucker never remembered a time before that incident. He never remembered one thing about his mother. We've all heard that children are resilient and bounce back pretty quickly after experiencing the death of a loved one. However, some children have a protective mechanism that the subconscious mind creates when there is something unbearable that has happened to them. It's a repressed memory, and most often it stays repressed.

Jack's dad ultimately remarried, and he had a good relationship with his stepmom, who also died when he was in his early twenties. He entered the army after high school, and then drove a taxicab in New York City while attending college to earn an electrical engineering degree.

Jack fell in love and married during that time, but he and his wife were both young and had different life dreams. She was ambitious and wanted to achieve certain goals in her life and she was ambitious for Jack as well. But all he wanted was to be a good engineer. For whatever reason, they divorced after a number of years. His ex-wife, Cookie, had severe osteoporosis and had surgery to replace bone marrow in her pelvis, which created unrelenting pain that she endured for many years. Jack stayed with her during her recovery after surgery even though we were together by then. But he wanted to help her during that difficult time. She still tried to create a good life for herself, but the quality of her life wasn't good and wasn't going to get better. Unfortunately she died from an accidental overdose of painkillers and alcohol when she was in her mid thirties. Jack had a wonderful relationship with Cookie's parents and her brother, Eddie, which stayed true all his life. Eddie always meant so much to Jack. He was the brother of his heart.

I met Jack when I was nineteen years old. He was an engineer at Northrop Corporation when I was working as a secretary for the night-shift supervisor. Jack had to do late-night testing, so we would see each other casually. I worked from 4 p.m. to midnight, and he left around 9 or 10 p.m.

Jack was a good-looking man who dressed impeccably and had a wonderful personality that attracted both men and women. He was the kind of person who could talk to anyone and learn all about them in twenty minutes. He was kind, funny, and a true gentleman. He never wanted to be more than a hands-on engineer, never wanted to be a supervisor or in charge of a project. He liked the creative process. He also had a quality of dignity that could be interpreted as aloofness. It made him appear authoritative and a bit disdainful of those he felt were not being authentic. I see that same dignity in our daughter. She also has a charismatic manner that draws people to her.

Jack and I started talking while at work and were very attracted to one another even though he was ten years older than me. We started meeting after work, then fell in love and got married four years later when I was twenty-three. The first time I brought him home to a family dinner where everyone called me "Cookie," I saw Jack turn white. He didn't know I had a nickname. How ironic that his first wife was nicknamed Cookie, too.

During that time, his career blossomed. He worked at the Jet Propulsion Laboratory on the project for the first soft landing on the moon, and he helped build the Shaker Lab at Goddard Space Flight Center. Later, he worked on the Deep Submergence Rescue Vehicle and spent many hours on a nuclear submarine. He was very successful.

After I married Jack, I was offered a position in the legal department of Twentieth Century Fox. I worked on artist, director, and producer contracts for about a year. But since I wanted to be involved in production, I went into the steno pool. The head of the department offered me a job working for a «very difficult» British director. She said if I took the job that after the film was completed, I could have my choice of any position I wanted.

In all of my working experience, this job was the most interesting. I liked the director, Michael Sarne. He was extremely creative, and he had his own vision that was in conflict with the producer's. The film was *Myra Breckenridge* and starred Raquel Welch as Myra. The costumes were amazing, and Raquel looked extremely beautiful in them. It was the first motion picture for Farrah Fawcett. And it also featured the great director, John Houston, in an acting role, and the extraordinary Mae West, who came out of retirement at seventy-six, or "seventy-sex" as she said.

Mae West insisted that only she could wear white or be a full blond, so no white-costume embellishments for Raquel, and no light-blond hair for Farrah. The film was such a kick. The movie was about a man who became a transgender woman (and this was in 1970!). The producer and Rex Reed, who played Myra's alter ego, appeared to be gay. Michael was straight. The director is always in charge of the film until the final cut. So Michael's vision won. But there was so much conflict between them with the producer bad-mouthing the film to the media.

Mae West wanted a leaning board to rest on with her long dresses, so Raquel wanted one, too. Raquel wasn't too happy about not being able to wear white, and there were some scenes she was very uncomfortable with. *Myra Breckenridge* was the first *X*-rated movie ever produced as it had some nudity and profanity in it. The film seems so innocent by today's standards! All the extras were nude and their bodies were painted to appear they were wearing bathing suits.

Also, per Mae West's contract, she had the right to write her own scenes since no one could do her type of dialogue as well as she could. So one of the highlights of my career was when she asked me to take dictation for her. She greeted me wearing a white silk top and pants, and of course she talked like Mae West. She always talked about herself in the third person: "Mae" would do this or that; it was never, "I" would do this or that. But it was fun. Michael, though, also had to put his stamp on it, ego being ego and all. But they compromised, and the scenes were funny.

With all of these good times, there was a dark side. Michael's wife, Tanya, was in the last quarter of her pregnancy when they were invited to visit a friend in Beverly Hills, but at the last minute something came up and they couldn't go. The next morning, we all heard about Sharon Tate and the Manson cult murders. That's who they were going to visit, and they were devastated.

Most evenings after the filming wrapped, a few people would come back to the office and party. There were always snacks, and people drank vodka and passed around a joint. I sometimes would have a drink, but never took a hit. I was offered so many pills by the handful. "Take your pick," I was told. I don't do drugs—never did—but there was a lot of it going around. We also had a lot of strange visitors.

With all of this, I did get my one and only chance to be in a movie. We were on the set, and a girl who was cast for a small part was to be replaced. She was the girlfriend of someone with a lot of influence at Twentieth Century Fox and they must have had a fight because she was asked not to come. I had a lot of friends in the crew, so the casting agent threw out this suggestion, "Why don't you cast Marie?" So Michael put me in for that small part. I was able to work with the outrageously wonderful horror movie king of the past, John Carradine. His hands were so twisted and arthritic, he had to be in a lot of pain. But he loved to tell stories on the set. He played the surgeon who was doing the transgender operation. I played the second nurse. There it is. My little bit of film experience and a very good memory.

Michael would say that he wasn't even able to cast his brother David in the film. Speaking of his brother, David wanted to write a tell-all story about all the infighting during the making of the movie. There was also a lot I didn't know about Raquel, David Brown, and Richard Zanuck, the CEO of Twentieth Century Fox. I only knew there were some problems, and David knew the full scoop. So Michael asked that I type out what his brother wrote.

Evidently, he must have passed something around because I got a strong notice from the steno pool administrator to stop all work for David. My typewriter only wrote in very large type which was recognizable, so I had to stop typing for him. I don't know if he ever wrote the book.

Once Michael started editing the film, his state of mind changed. He became very extravagant with the film and put in a lot of cuts of Laurel and Hardy and slapstick comedy. This was a movie that was truly over the top and you couldn't really figure it out. However, it became a cult film.

As the film was ending, there was a big Screen Actors Guild strike in 1970, the largest of its kind. If the actors don't work, no one else does, either. Twentieth Century Fox laid off most of its production people, and I was one of the last to go. The *Hollywood Reporter* had a full page ad for *Myra Breckenridge* showing all of the actors in a room with Michael lying down on the floor in front of them. The title of the ad was, "Togetherness." I framed it and had Michael sign it. His signature is faded now, but I still have the picture in my office because it makes me feel good.

Since I was not working any longer, it seemed a good time to consider having a family. Not long after that our daughter, Nichole Royale Drucker, was born. I remember how Jack painted her room so carefully and put up pictures on the wall, and right after she was born, he put a radio near her crib so she wouldn't feel alone. He loved her so much and cuddled and played with her as often as he could. He was one of those dads who changed diapers and bathed the babies. I was so fortunate.

Two years later in 1973, I was eight months pregnant with our son, and that is where I began this book, with Jack in the hospital.

He was working in San Diego on a submarine during the week. He came home on Friday nights and left early Monday mornings. One day, he came home and complained of feeling light-headed and dizzy. I noticed that his skin was yellow and wanted him to go to the emergency room. But he said it was nothing and it would go away. That night, our good friends, Micki and Joe Picchiotti, came over to visit with us, and I told them how Jack said he felt, which he acknowledged, and asked them what they thought about his color. They were alarmed as well and insisted they drive us to the emergency room. By then, we had convinced Jack that we didn't like what we saw.

We were fortunate. That night, the doctor on call was a nephrologist who specialized in kidney problems. He took one look at Jack's blood work and told us that Jack needed to be admitted to the hospital immediately. His blood pressure was so high that he was a walking stroke waiting to happen. Jack bargained with him and said he would admit himself to the hospital the next morning.

We all went out to dinner that night and discussed how crazy life can be, and we were worried. The next day, Jack was admitted to the hospital, and the doctor told us that Jack had only 5 percent kidney function, and he had to have surgery immediately so they could put him on dialysis.

Here is where "Life Interrupted" began. The story continues here, after he passed out. Jack was unconscious, and the doctor was calling his name and lightly slapping his cheek. I was huddled in the corner of the hospital room, mesmerized by the kidney dialysis machine and frightened out of my wits while nurses and doctors seemed to be running all over the place. Finally, Jack returned to consciousness, but it seemed to take forever. Jack called it "going down the tubes," and I never wanted it to happen again, and neither did he.

The doctors told us that because he only had a 5 percent function of his kidneys, he would need to be on dialysis the rest of his life. The cost would be prohibitive. Our only choice was to go on Medicaid, which meant we had to sell our house because you are not allowed to own anything other than a car and furniture. We were fortunate that our neighbor wanted a rental property, so we sold the house to him and rented it back from him. Not too long after that, we were told that the VA would take care of Jack because he had been in the Korean War and was married with small children. In those days, dialysis was rare, and many people needing it couldn't get it. Unfortunately, we had already sold our house. But fortunately, we would not be paupers, and Jack could continue working at his career when he recovered.

Jack was stoic and very noble about the great change happening in his body and his life. He never complained, always complied with his medical instructions, and did his best to get on with life. I'm sure he had very bad moments, but he didn't let me see them. He was very concerned about my pregnancy and the upcoming birth of our child.

During this nightmarish time, I gave birth to a son, Chad Aron Drucker. We were not able to finish our Lamaze classes, and Jack wasn't even sure if he could be there when our child was born if it were on a day he was having dialysis. In those days, dialysis took *six hours*. But the sun shined on us, and Jack was with me in the delivery room for the natural birth of our son Chad.

I was nursing Chad and had to run to the hospital to train to be a dialysis assistant because the goal was to have the machine in our home. It took six weeks for me to complete the training, and Jack was just getting used to the dialysis himself. This was before the time breast milk could be pumped and saved, so my sister, Millie, lived with us and took care of Chad while I ran to the hospital and back. I was so grateful for her. Not only did she try to comfort Chad when he was hungry if I didn't get back in time but she also prepared meals for us that were low in salt and protein for Jack's special dietary needs.

While in training, I'll never forget the first time I had to take the cannula and split it so I could hook him up to both sides of the dialysis machine. I literally held Jack's life in my hands. I cared deeply for this man and was holding his actual lifeline. I can see why doctors don't perform surgery on loved ones. It is just too personal, too meaningful.

In the meantime, the VA had a technician set up a dialysis machine and all the equipment and medical supplies in our home. We had sterile pads, blood pressure monitoring devices, tubes, needles, lines of vinyl tubing, tapes, saline bags, heparin tubes along with medications and a huge barrel of dialyasate. We also had our own reverse osmosis machine. My God, we practically had a mini-hospital!

After six weeks at the hospital, the first time I put him on the machine at home, we had a supervisor watching me, and everything went very well. The second time, I almost killed him. The normal way to bring someone off the machine is to hang a bag of saline and attach it to the tube the needle is in so that air doesn't get into the person. However, Jack didn't like the additional fluid, so he didn't want me to attach the bag. Taking a person off a dialysis machine in those days required clamping a hemostat, unclamping another hemostat, then clamping again so no air would get into the bloodstream.

Well, I clamped, unclamped, and dropped the hemostat on the floor. I bent over to grab it, but it was hard to grasp it with my sterile gloves, and I fumbled a bit before I got it back in my hand. By the time I looked up, the pump showed Jack was just twelve inches from getting air in his artery. I quickly clamped, turned white, and had to sit down or I would have fainted. I never got over it. For the four years he dialyzed at home, I would concentrate, hold my breath, clamp, unclamp, clamp—and breathe. It always scared the hell out of me to take him off the machine.

Northrop gave Jack a job in the San Fernando Valley. He had been commuting to San Diego and working on a submarine before he got ill. When he returned to work, the rat race started; we felt like rats running around in a circle. Jack dialyzed three times a week— Tuesday, Thursday, and Saturday. On Tuesdays and Thursdays around 5 p.m., I would set up the machine and prime all the tubing with saline. I would then set up a sterile field with the needles, tubes, and other medications Jack would need. This took about an hour. After that, I started preparing dinner and made sure Chad was fed.

When Jack came home, he would change into more comfortable clothing, wash up and sit in the recliner, and I would clean his arm with alcohol pads, separate the tubes of his cannula, and connect him to the prepped machine, then turn it on. When he was first diagnosed, both of his arms were operated on. A cannula was put in one arm and a fistula in the other. A cannula is twelve inches of tubing. One end is affixed to an artery going in one direction, and the other end is affixed to the artery going in the other direction. Somehow, the magic of surgery and the superb knowledge of the surgeons make this happen. The cannula can then be split in the middle to connect each side to tubing that is connected to the dialysis machine. As this is an external device, once removed from the machine, the cannula needs to be wrapped to the arm to prevent it from being accidently damaged.

The other arm has this same type of connection made internally so that it can be accessed by a needle directly through the skin. This is called a fistula. Jack's fistula took months to heal before it was ready to use.

After he was hooked up, I would feed him and Nichole. She was only twenty-two months old, and Chad was just a few weeks old. We all stayed in the dialysis room and watched TV. Jack needed to have his blood pressure taken every hour. There were a lot of alarms on the machine that would signal me if there was a problem, so I had to stay diligent. And boy, when one went off, I would get an adrenalin rush. I didn't want Jack to go "down the tubes" in front of me.

Jack would get on the machine by 6 p.m., and I would take him off at midnight. He would then clean everything with formaldehyde so he could reuse the tubes. This would take him an hour. Then he would get ready for bed and try to sleep. It always took time for him to settle down to sleep even though he had to get up by 6 a.m. The baby would wake me up every three or four hours to nurse, so I didn't get much sleep, either. The good thing was at least I didn't have to deal with baby bottles and formula. Jack became allergic to the formaldehyde after a few months. His whole body was one painful, red, burning, itching hive. Finally, the VA consented to give him fresh tubing for each dialysis session.

Jack liked his job but felt that he couldn't give it his all because he couldn't travel to the Middle East like the other members of his team needed to do. However, he was very grateful to have a job even if he didn't get much sleep and was often weak.

After seven months of this strange ritual, Jack wanted to visit his dad and sisters in New York. He went alone as the cost was prohibitive for all four of us to go. While on the plane, I got a call that a kidney had been found for him, and transplant surgery scheduled. They needed him immediately. I told the specialist at the hospital that Jack was on a flight to New York and gave them his flight information. Unbelievably, when the pilot received this information, he turned the plane around and returned to the airport where Jack was picked up and taken directly to the hospital to have immediate surgery. It became a news item in the papers.

The kidney transplant was successful, and everything was going well. Jack was so happy he glowed, and we talked about how we would travel and be free to do whatever we wanted. Jack could produce urine again, and I think he imagined himself peeing everywhere, writing his name in the dirt and on walls, and so on. Over time, dialysis stops urine production, tear production, and all bodily produced fluids dry up. Thankfully, it happens gradually, so a person has time to get used to it, but it is very hard to go through.

After about a week, still in the hospital, Jack started hiccupping nonstop, and the doctors told him his body might be rejecting the kidney, but they were giving him a lot of medicine to try and stop the rejection process. After a few days of terrible discomfort, he was told his body had rejected the transplanted kidney, and he was taken to surgery to have it removed.

(This is the hard part and makes me weep even now so many years later.) After the surgery, I went into Jack's room and put my arms around him. He said, "They've taken my kidney," and he just sobbed in my arms. I don't ever remember Jack crying before or since that time. We had been so happy, so elated, and the rug was ripped out from under us.

The grief was terrible for both of us. The fall from exultation to reality was unbelievably hard. Where do you go from here? I held him and told him he didn't need to go back to work. We didn't need to be running around in circles any longer. He had a disability, and it was time for both of us to face it and allow ourselves time to heal. Fortunately, Jack had long-term disability coverage from Northrop, and Social Security kicked in, so we had a limited but good-enough income.

We were able to purchase another home, and the VA moved all the dialysis equipment into it. We continued dialysis in our home and became a world unto ourselves, just the four of us.

During this time, my mother's cancer had progressed. Jack's failed transplant was in August, and Mom died in October. I was still nursing Chad and couldn't allow myself the full range of grief I felt because I thought it would transfer to Chad. I had to make myself stay as serene as I could both for Jack's and Chad's sakes.

We all have mixed emotions about grief after a loved one dies from a terminal illness after having suffered so long and the quality of life is nil. Personally, I started grieving for my mother the day I heard the cancer was terminal. She was very ill at the same time Jack went through the whole kidney transplant process. I was visiting her in one hospital and him in the other. She was in constant pain and her passing was a blessing. I really missed her light, her encouragement and love. I miss it to this day.

But I could not allow myself to go to that dark place that grief can drive us to. I couldn't control the grief wave, but there were too many people who relied on me to be strong, and so the strength came from somewhere inside of me. I believe in the Almighty, the Divine Creator, God, and I turned over my worry and grief to prayer. I personally believe we are all connected by this great Divine Intelligence. We're all just lots of atoms and molecules moved by an Intelligent Force that imparts to each of us a spiritual essence, a personality.

I think the grief process makes us look at our spiritual beliefs, and during grief, connecting to our spiritual side can help comfort us.

So Jack continued to dialyze at home for a number of years, then I decided we needed to be part of the outside world and convinced him to dialyze at the VA hospital while I started doing temporary work that ended up being full time. It was good for him to be with other people. He started a routine of playing cards with another inmate. Sorry, I mean another patient named Gil. I forgot myself for a moment because Jack and Gil were prisoners to their dialysis machines. You go on it or you die. Gil and Jack became very close over the years, and the nurses were part of their family as well. The nurses get close to their patients in this particular setting.

Jack would be home by 1 p.m. on the days he dialyzed, so he was there for the kids. We had a role reversal that took time for him to become accustomed to. It angered him that I was working and he had to stay at home, prepare meals, and take care of the kids. Finally, he surrendered to it, thankfully. He made it okay within himself to be a stay-at-home dad.

After about seven years of living like this, Jack started having very strange episodes of blacking out without warning. He would be standing talking to me and the next moment be on the ground. The doctors couldn't figure out what was wrong. One time, Chad saw Jack pass out. Jack had just brought the bicycle in from outside and threw himself over the sofa and passed out. Chad ran for the nitroglycerin and ran to put it under Jack's tongue. We had 911 signs next to each telephone for the kids. Jack's quality of life sucked according to him, and he told me that if they couldn't find out what was wrong, he didn't want to live like this.

We were invited to an evening pool party by our friends. There were about eight of us having a good time. Jack had a CAT scan earlier that day. As we were ready to leave, everyone hugged and held him. It was strange, but in retrospect, they were all saying good-bye.

I still remember the day I watched him in the living room from our foyer. I leaned against the wall filled with love for him and knew I wouldn't have him long.

Jack was coaching Little League for Chad, and one day in the dugout, Chad reached up, gave Jack a kiss, and then Jack fell off the bench face down on the dirt. I got a call at work that he had a heart attack, and I rushed from work to the hospital, thinking all the way, "Please let him be okay, please let him be okay." He was in the emergency room waiting to be transferred to the VA when I walked in. His eyes were so big and blue, and he had dirt smeared on his nose and face. He was scared. He told me that he had felt a great pressure and tremendous pain in his chest right before he fell off the bench. He said he never wanted to feel something like that again.

He was transferred and settled in at the VA hospital and it took a long time before they let me see him. I stayed in the waiting room with Eddie, Jack's brother-in-law from his previous marriage, who was there for both of us. The policy of the hospital was to keep a heart attack victim in the hospital for ten days for observation. Jack would still have the occasional blackout, and he was given a heart monitor to wear 24/7. After a few days, I took the kids to see him, and they brought him fresh cherries to eat. They needed to see him, and Chad needed to know that his kiss didn't cause the heart attack. Jack wanted to be with the children, too. He didn't sleep well, so he would roam the halls and get into deep conversations with the night staff. Many of the nurses already knew him. He was charming and could get them to talk about anything.

Jack had been in the hospital for about six days when I received a phone call at 7 a.m., and the doctor told me Jack had another heart attack. They tried to revive him for forty-five minutes, but he died. The doctor was shaken and wrenched from the effort and told me he was very sorry for my loss. I could feel his sadness. I hung up and started sobbing and tried to get myself together so I could tell the kids. I didn't realize it until many years later when Nichole told me she heard me crying and went downstairs and looked into the bathroom mirror and told herself her daddy was dead; she already knew when I told her. She had swiftly gone back to her bed and pretended to be asleep. I went to her and told her and held her as she cried. Then I went to Chad's room, woke him, and told him.

We were all so numb and grief-stricken that none of us remembers much of that day or the days following. My good friends, Micki and Joe, took me to the hospital to get Jack's things, and I made arrangements for his funeral, which needed to be done the next day according to his religious beliefs. We had a memorial service, and I just couldn't look into the casket. I only wanted to remember Jack alive because my last memory of my mom was seeing her in a casket and that memory haunted me. I had Joe and my niece's husband, John, look in to make sure it was Jack. I wanted to know he was there, but I just couldn't look. He was a vet, so he had a military funeral with the American flag draped over the casket, and at the burial site, someone wrapped it up and presented to me.

I remember during the memorial service my minister saying that I had to let him go, not hold on, but let him go into the light. I hated her for years for telling me that. I've since forgiven her and myself, but this is a good example of bad advice after the death of a loved one.

A few weeks later, still a bit dazed, I was taking a walk in my neighborhood. I even remember the chalk marks made in the middle of the street by surveyors with big yellow arrows pointing in different directions. I had walked about a mile, and then stopped at that curb where those yellow arrows were, and I said, "Good-bye, Jack." And I let him go like my minister said to do. This was the hardest thing I have ever done and caused me the most grief. And it was so unnecessary. It is never necessary to let go. Our loved ones stay around us and many of us talk to them as it brings us peace and solace. Unfortunately, I didn't realize this until much later, and I suffered for my decision to follow my minister's ill advice.

Jack's death was sudden. I didn't really expect it. In my mind, I would still see him come down the stairs, grinning at me. How does one just disappear, to go from something solid to nothing? It's unreal. Death seems unreal. The only reality is that they are definitely gone.

And one by one, my support group disappeared. My niece and her husband moved to New Jersey. Jack's sister's daughter, my niece, died in a head-on car collision one month to the day of Jack's death. Both of my sisters lived in Hawaii, and my closest friends, Micki and Joe, moved to Chicago. We were a small family, and they were all gone. The kids and I were alone. Thankfully, we had hired Helen, our live-in nanny, a couple of weeks before Jack died. She was there to help with the children while I worked.

I struggled with how I was to go on. I took two weeks off from work, and after I went back, when a grief wave hit me, I'd run to the bathroom and sob, but I'm sure everyone could hear me. And there was nothing I could do about it. I couldn't control it. We all need a Wailing Wall, and I guess that was mine. After two months, I remember one of my coworkers telling me I had to snap myself out of it and get on with my life and stop feeling sorry for myself. Someone else implied that I had wallowed in grief so long that it was tedious. That's when I knew I had to quit. I needed peace and tranquility where no one judged me. Fortunately for me, Jack had life insurance, so I could take time off from work to heal.

That was a big lesson for me. People who have not experienced grief themselves have no concept of it. They don't know how to offer comfort or what to say. Obviously, I was angry at them for judging me. I still was numb and not thinking clearly. I just needed a place to hide and heal my wounds. I was angry at my minister, my coworkers, and myself. Plus, I felt abandoned by my only support group. There was no one I could call on for help or to talk to. I didn't realize that there were free hospice grief support groups. Maybe they didn't even exist then as they do now.

It was a difficult year. Jack died in June, and my older sister, Millie, had her leg amputated in October. Her arteries had hardened and the blood flow closed down. My other sister, Betty, had her leg amputated in November. She had an infected little toe that the doctor ignored until it was too late. When was this dark cloud going to go away? It was too much. I couldn't stand it. You know how you feel when you just can't stand it? Was I going to fracture? So I had to reach down deep inside myself and find a spiritual solace. It is there if you look. We are more than our bodies. I connected to help from the Holy Spirit. That's what I call it anyway. And I was able to go on. My children were nine and seven; we all had to heal together.

A few days after Jack died, I remember sitting by Chad's bed. He was laying with his head on a pillow with his hands behind his head, and he couldn't stop crying; tears were running down his face. He told me he had so many tears in him that his pillow was going to get all wet. I guess that sums it up for all of us.

So, how did I cope? It was hard. I missed Jack in bed and in my life. The children missed him. He was funny and loving, but I had to go on. When I heard that my sister, Betty, also was going to have her leg amputated, I remember that I just put my head down on the table sobbing, wondering what was going on and how I was going to get through all this grief and sadness. I remember that was the first time I actually turned it over to God. I felt that I couldn't cope by myself. I reached for that "Presence" within me, my God source, and asked for help to get through it all. I knew I couldn't do it on my own.

My friend took me to Carmel by the sea. The vastness of the ocean helped sooth my soul. I walked and felt the wind on my face. I tried to stay in the moment.

I still dream about Jack to this day. In my dream, every time I ask about why he isn't staying with me, I can't get a straight answer. In my dream, it seems that only his brother-in-law Eddie knows his telephone number.

In thinking back to that time about how I coped, I realized that I didn't know how or where to go to find help. I didn't know about grief groups. There was no Internet or other places I could find that I knew about. So now I say, reach out. Go to grief groups to be with others going through what you are. Share your feelings. Many of these groups are free.

Here are some Internet sources:

http://www.griefhealingdiscussiongroups.com/
www.facebook.com/mygriefsupport
www.griefhaven.org
www.compassionatefriends.org
www.griefshare.org

Chapter 11

My Sister Millie— In Pieces

My oldest sister was born Mildred Mary Martz, and she was very ill as a child. Millie was thirteen years older than me, and Betty was eleven years older.

Millie's life was difficult. I think in retrospect, she was bipolar. She could be so mean and would beat Betty up without conscience when they were teenagers. Betty was afraid of her when they went to school together, and she would cross to the other side of the street if Millie were walking toward her. After one big fight, Betty packed her bags and wanted to leave. She was in her early teens. My grandmother, Baba, talked her out of it, and she and Mom made Millie apologize and vow never to hurt her again. The bipolar part was that Millie could be very kind and loving. She was like a Dr. Jekyll, Mr. Hyde. Good or terrible. And when she was terrible, she was unreasonable. She carried an inner anger in her soul all her life.

My mom told me stories of how a babysitter punished Millie when she was young by cutting off all her long hair. I also remember the story of her stepfather, Nick, tying her spread-eagled to a bed and spanking her when she was fourteen. Really? Mom left him not long after that.

Millie never trusted men, and when she finally got married as a virginal bride at thirty-four to a small man named Pee Wee Purser, he left her two weeks after the ceremony and didn't return for three months. Then he took her to the Salton Sea and opened up a bar–diner with her as the cook. After a couple of years, he cut all the wires on her car and took off forever in his own car, totally abandoning her. She never saw him again. I'll never forget when Millie called Mom up on the phone, sobbing, and told us Pee Wee had left her. Mom, Jack, and I went to see her right away. She lay on my mom's lap on the couch and sobbed and sobbed. She never really recovered her confidence after that and certainly not in men.

But Millie was a different soul than many. She didn't know how to be responsible. When she took her first job for the telephone company after high school, she would charge up shopping trips and never pay the bills. She was let go after a few years because her creditors were garnishing her wages. She was in her early twenties by then, and she just gave up on finding a job and did nothing. When we all lived together, Mom would give Millie cash to pay a utility bill, and the electricity would go off. When she was asked why the bill wasn't paid, Millie said she wanted to buy some magazines. Mom also bought her a car with Millie's promise to make the payments. That lasted a few months, and then the car was repossessed. She just didn't get it that she needed to be responsible. When asked about helping to pay the rent, her attitude was, "Well, you have to pay for rent anyway." Never mind that Mom and I slept in one room, and she had a second bedroom all to herself. Mom couldn't say no to her. I think even Mom was afraid of her moods.

I remember when I was a little girl, Millie took me to have lunch with her at work. I was so proud, excited, and happy to be going out with her to lunch, but all she did was tell me to stop squirming around and that she would never take me out again to lunch because I couldn't behave. I still remember that day because it made me feel so bad. She was a strict disciplinarian.

I was terrified of my sister when I was young because she would constantly threaten to throw me against the wall or do something equally violent. She only hit me twice across the face that I can remember, but her threats frightened me. She became the authority figure in my life.

But there were also a lot of times Millie would cuddle me and I felt her love. That is what was so weird about her personality. I did love her, but I feared her, too.

The best thing my mom did was move with me to Pomona, California when I was twelve. Millie stayed with Betty, my grandmother, and Betty's husband at the time, Mel. I was able to blossom and enjoy my eighth and ninth grades. I went to football games and enjoyed my friends.

When I was fourteen, Mom moved back to Torrance, and Millie moved back in with Mom and me. One night I was going out with some friends, and as I welcomed them in, Millie started berating me for wearing eye makeup and telling me how terrible I looked and insisted I wash it off. I was so humiliated in front of my friends, and when we went out, I can only imagine what they thought. They were not happy about what had happened and tried to cheer me up.

When I was sixteen, I brought my girlfriend home with me from school, and Millie immediately started yelling at me that I hadn't run the sweeper and cleaned up the house. Understand that she had been home all day and wasn't working. She just kept getting angrier and angrier, and then told me to go to my room. She would be there in a minute to deal with me. My girlfriend went home. Do you know what it means to "see red"? I never felt that kind of anger in my life before or since. My aura of anger must have filled the whole room, because I knew that I was going to kill my sister. I was ready to fight with her and throw us both out the window, and I didn't care if I died in the process. She opened the door, must have felt my huge anger, and said, "Don't you ever do that again," in a weak little voice, and shut the door.

We moved again, and Mom found Millie a job taking "book" over our phone, which was strictly illegal. My mom loved to gamble on the horses, and she knew bookies. Millie would be on the phone taking racetrack bets, writing them down on our kitchen table, then calling the "bookie" and giving him the information. She would then sponge off the ceramic table and repeat the process. She did this for about a year, then one day I came home from high school and saw the lock broken on the front door, which was slightly ajar. When I walked in, I saw Millie sitting on the couch surrounded by police officers. She was sent to jail for six months. When she got out, she would pace in an 8' x 8' pattern for months after that.

I remember another time just before I was graduated from high school. Mom's friend was making me a beautiful prom dress, and Millie just lost it there in front of Mom's friend and me. She started yelling at me; her rage was so great that it was way over-the-top unreasonable. I don't know if it was because I was going to the prom and she had never gone, or what. I think she even scared my mom's friend.

Millie's friends never saw the crazy part of her. She could be kind and fun, and when she went out drinking with her friends, she often brought them home in the early hours and made everyone breakfast. She truly had two personalities.

As I became a responsible adult, Millie recognized the change in me and treated me differently. One of the kindest things she ever did was to stay with us during the time Jack was diagnosed with kidney failure right after I gave birth to Chad. That was such a trying time for all of us, but she took care of the home, cooked for us, and handled Chad and Nichole with such love and respect. I hold this memory very dearly in my heart.

She had mellowed a lot by then unless something displeased her. She was working at a telephone answering service and living with Mom and my Niece Vicki at the time. She was about forty-two years old then. She was a smoker like the rest of my family and had to have bypass surgery.

After Mom died, Millie, Betty, and Vicki all moved to Hawaii where Betty wanted to bury her husband's ashes. Millie stayed there for twelve years.

In 1980, Jack died in June, and Millie had hardening of the arteries so severely that in October she had one leg amputated below the knee and the toes amputated on the other foot. In November, I got a call from my sister Betty that her small toe had gotten infected, and the doctor had neglected her to the point that her foot was turning dark, and she was in great pain up to her ankle. I told her I would get on a plane and come to her immediately, but she said she was seeing a doctor the next day. The next thing I knew, she also had her leg amputated below the knee. All this happened the last half of the year, and I finally thought I was having a nervous breakdown. It was just too much. I grieved for their losses as well as for Jack. How do you get through this? I didn't know I had so many tears in me.

The following July, I traveled to Hawaii to see them after their rehabilitation. Betty greeted me at the airport walking with her prosthetic leg. I was so moved and so proud of her. She took me to their home, and Millie lovingly greeted me on crutches. They were both funny, though. As soon as they got home, both of them removed their legs and sat in their wheelchairs. It prompted me to think of the Wheelchair Minuet. It was a dance they did around one another. Both of them had such good attitudes. I never saw them feeling despondent, but I know they must have suffered terribly. I was there a week with them, and it was wonderful.

In 1984, Betty and Millie moved back to California and stayed with me, and then later they moved in together in a home close by. In 1986, Milled suffered a stroke, which affected her mind. She could no longer read, and how she loved to read! And she lost all her aggression. Only mild Millie remained. It was like she had a lobotomy. In 1987, I took her to the doctor to check out a small dark spot on the leg where she had no toes. We heard the terrible news that it was gangrene. It quickly moved up her leg, and she consented to have the leg amputated up to the hip. After the surgery, she was so happy to be able to come home, and we were all going to celebrate. But the stitches wouldn't heal, and the doctors said she had no blood flow below her kidneys. They tried to put in a stent, but it didn't work. And they had to move her to a convalescent home that cared for large, open wounds. She stayed there for many months. She was full of pain meds and was almost unaware when we visited. And we couldn't come often because we now lived in San Diego, and she was in Los Angeles.

The next year, I received a call from Millie's doctor telling me that she had gangrene in the other leg, the one with the previous amputation below the knee. He wanted to know whether to operate. I was devastated and asked him if it would be more painful to amputate or to let the gangrene take her. He said it was about the same, so I told him to let her go. Let her find peace. She died within the week. (It was such a difficult decision, and I'm crying while writing this. I can't normally even talk about her death without crying.) She died after being taken apart piece by piece and living in her own hell. I felt guilty for letting her go but happy she was finally at peace and free again.

Now, I'm glad I made that decision. Sometimes, we have to make hard decisions and live with the consequences, but I wanted her to live and have quality in her life, and since that wasn't possible, I didn't want her to merely exist and live in pain without love around her. She was released to go Home. No more pain or suffering.

Chapter 12

Chad—Beloved Son and Brother

Chad was the gift that I received during the difficult part of my life when I found out about Jack's illness and Mom's cancer. Everything was in turmoil, but Chad kept me calm and sane because I was breastfeeding him and needed to feel at peace when doing it. My precious twenty-two-month-old daughter was my joy, and the two of them kept my life in balance.

When Chad was very little, about three years old, he came to our bed in the middle of the night and told me he was scared. The "soul" people were in his room. Now, I never mentioned that word to him, ever. So I asked him what they looked like, and he said white. They didn't hurt him, but he was frightened of them. I told him they were probably watching over him to keep him safe, but he still wanted to stay with us.

A few months after I started a steady relationship with my second husband John, there was a poignant moment when both John and Chad were lying on the floor with one knee crossed over the other. Chad was only eight. John is a very funny man and had charmed Chad with his kindness. So bit by bit, Chad scooted closer to John, then he plopped his head on John's shoulder. It was so sweet. The two of them were very similar in likes and temperament and became good buddies over the years. I'm thankful John was able to be such a good stepfather. They truly loved one another.

Chad was extremely good-looking, charming, and very kind, and the girls loved him. John and I came home from work one day and saw six or seven bicycles on our lawn. When we went into the house, Chad was sitting in the middle of a group of his "friends"; there were three girls on his right and three girls on his left. He greeted us with, "Hi Mom, hi John. These are my friends."

He also did beautiful stained-glass work. It was his hobby, and some of my friends still have his work.

As Chad got older, after Jack died, he started having nightmares. He'd dream of tigers and bees coming after him, and he'd go lay down on the floor next to Nichole's bed or fall asleep right in front of our bedroom door. He always had circles under his eyes from lack of sleep, and I was worried.

He was also having a lot of trouble in school because, even as early as second grade, he would never do his homework. He could read and do workbooks with me before he started kindergarten, but he just couldn't write.

Chad was very bright. At eleven, he tested high in statistical thinking. He could put together any involved puzzle in seconds. He was able to read from the age of three, but his problem was that he couldn't write so he couldn't do his homework. He was behind in small-motor development according to more school tests, and he was also dyslexic and wrote numbers and letters backward. He just saw things differently. He had a wonderful teacher when he was eleven who understood his needs, and he blossomed, but we had to move, and the teachers in the new school didn't try to take the time to understand him.

Once we moved, the new teacher didn't realize he had a learning problem and just thought he was a troublemaker. He was put into special education classes, and the teacher, Mr. Swisher, told him he would never amount to anything. Why would a teacher say something like that?

It was close to the end of the school year, and I was called to school at a roundtable discussion where everyone told me how bad and wrong my child was. They hadn't even looked at his medical tests and just felt he wasn't trying. In addition, I found out years later after we moved to San Diego that Chad and a few of his school friends went to a man's house after school because the man told them he would teach them how to work with cars. This was a ruse, and the man molested all of the children at one time or another. He actually went to the school, claimed he was Chad's dad, and took him out of school to his home. This is the same school that gave me such a hard time about Chad's behavior. I didn't find out about this until Chad was sixteen. He had dealt with it in his own way and had stayed away from that pervert after he was molested.

Canyon Country Elementary School is near Valencia, California. There was nothing I could do so many years later, and I didn't even know the man's name.

As the kids got older, my rule was they had to be in by 11 p.m., and they had to knock on my bedroom door and tell me they were home, whether I was asleep or not. They knew I couldn't sleep well otherwise. But often one or the other would see a light on under the door and they knew I was reading. They would knock, then open the door and come and sit down on the side of the bed and tell me about their day. They both knew that I would always put down my book and give them my undivided attention, and we had wonderful quality time together. That seemed to be their time, and we would talk about anything and everything. At first the kids would whisper, but it would wake John, who complained about the whispering. It drove him nuts. But if everyone talked in their normal voices, he was fine and just kept on sleeping.

When I was growing up, my family had always ignored me if they were reading or watching TV and would shush me when I wanted to talk. It hurt my feelings, so I vowed I would never do that to my children. Nichole told me when she was older how much it meant to them that I would always stop whatever I was doing and give them my undivided attention.

In Chad's last year of school, he was having a very hard time with the special education teachers. I really don't think they cared at all, and he was discouraged, humiliated, and felt he wasn't as good as other people. I absolutely could not have him believing that way about himself, so since he was over sixteen, I allowed him to leave school with their permission.

John helped him gt a job as a car stereo installer, and he did it very well. It was the craftsman in him. He started to feel good about himself again and regained his confidence. He felt he had a career that would continue to pay him well, and in time, I felt he would probably go to school again, probably to learn electronics because John had taught him so much already. He just needed time to heal and grow into himself as a man.

Unfortunately, his friends and coworkers also exposed him to drugs and alcohol, and Chad went through a difficult period. After a frightening episode with drugs, Chad realized his behavior was out of control. He started backing away from the friends he had who were into such self-destructive behavior.

Chad turned eighteen and had a new girlfriend that he really liked. He wanted to straighten out for her and for himself as well. He decided to purchase his own car, and then he took the first ride with his friend to the desert to try it out. They had a few beers and stayed out there quite a while. Chad felt really good about himself and was in a great place.

I got the phone call at 7 a.m. the next morning. We had a security gate, and the caller said he was the coroner and could he come in. I buzzed him in and went to the door as he knocked. The word "coroner" never sunk in.

He asked, "Is this the home of Chad Drucker?"

"Yes," I said.

"Does he drive a red Hyundai?"

"Yes."

"I'm very sorry to inform you that your son was in an accident."

My adrenaline started to surge, and I was confused. "Is he okay?" I asked.

"No, he isn't." "

Are you trying to tell me that he's dead?"

"Yes."

"Where is he?"

"He's in the hospital."

"But I thought you said he was dead."

"He is. He's in the morgue."

This conversation took place so fast, and my mind was whirling, then I finally got it. I started to gasp and gasp and gasp and gasp. The coroner gently pushed me back into the house so I would sit down and not faint.

My sister Betty yelled to my daughter, "Nichole, wake up. Chad's dead." In the back of my mind, I knew that was such a terrible way to tell her. Betty must have overheard the conversation. John was out. He'd taken a friend to the airport for an early flight.

Betty, Nichole, and I were all crying as we sat around the coroner. He told us that Chad had taken a curve too fast onto the freeway, and his car had rolled. He went out the window and the car landed on him, crushing him. He wasn't wearing a seatbelt. His passenger, Jeremy, survived without a scratch because he was wearing one.

This happened at 1 a.m., and Jeremy looked all over for Chad, calling him, and finally saw that he was under the car. He searched for a callbox and finally got the police to the accident site.

The coroner was a very kind man. I asked if I could see Chad, but he told me it wasn't a good idea for me to see him that way. His body had already been identified by Jeremy and Jeremy's father. I remember a moment feeling that Chad was with me, almost as though he had his hands on my shoulders, saying, "I'm right here, Mom." I also felt Jack right beside him. It was surreal.

Then the coroner shook out a large envelope that had Chad's wallet, car keys, and some other mementos that he carried with him. He told me that I could contact the morgue and have Chad's body removed by a funeral home. Then he left.

Obviously, we were all in a daze, crying and carrying on. When John came home, we had to tell him what happened. My mind was so clouded and in shock at the time that I don't remember exactly what we did. I remember that later Jeremy and his dad came by. Jeremy looked terrible in his grief and tried his best to console us.

We had Chad cremated, and I thought I would have a small memorial service, but Chad's friends took that right out of my hands. I had to set a date at a church, and it was filled. Well over one hundred people were there, mostly Chad's school friends and coworkers.

That was such a difficult time to go through. I lit a candle with his picture next to it with some flowers and a love note from his girlfriend that I set on a cabinet in the living room so we could look at them. I think we must have lit that candle for at least a year. It stayed in our bathroom, and the flickering light gave me comfort.

Anyone who has lost a child knows what that gut-wrenching feeling is like. The grief is so hard and deep and very difficult to go through. Actually, it's unbearable. But sometimes I would feel him with me, almost touching me, and I would have momentary peace. It was as if he were saying, "I'm right here, Mom. I'm holding you. It's okay." We also experienced a lot of paranormal events that I will talk about in the last chapter.

I was feeling very down and starting to feel sorry for myself when a friend recommended that I speak to a woman named Olive who was some kind of psychic. We spoke for a while, and I told her what had happened, then she said she understood because she had been in an automobile accident and lost her husband and her son, and she was paralyzed from the waist down. I no longer remember what we talked about after she told me that, but when I hung up, my pity party was over, and I was so glad I wasn't her. It helped me put my life in perspective.

I was concerned about Nichole. She was grieving and I didn't know how to help her. I even told her that I didn't know how I could get through this and go on living. She said, "Mom, you still have me." Oh, how I didn't mean to hurt her even more. I have the most wonderful daughter. She lights up my heart every time I see or hear her. I tried to reassure her how much she meant to me. That it was just my grief talking and not what I really meant. I told her that I hoped her boyfriend held her when the grief hit hard. I held her. But I was pretty useless at comforting anyone at that point.

Nichole said that she tried to find a book about the death of a brother, but never did see one. I'm going to put this in her own words so that anyone who wants to know what others have gone through when a brother dies might feel some comfort.

> "I really wanted to read about someone who experienced the loss of a brother and how they got through it. I remember saying, "I hate you, Chad," when we fought. It's natural for a brother and sis-

ter to fight, but that's something I remembered when Chad died.

"When you are young like this, you feel embarrassed that your peers, your friends will judge you. So you try to hide it and pretend everything is okay. I was so sad, and it was so hard, but I wanted to hear about somebody who got through my kind of grief. I wanted to be reassured I could get through this…but there were no books available. There was no Internet in those days or social media where Chad's friends might have expressed their feelings. But it wasn't there for me.

"You don't want your friends to look at you with pity or feel sorry for you. It's different when you are young. I felt uncomfortable and different. I was searching for my own solace and couldn't find anything that could give me that.

"I didn't feel I had anyone to cry with. My friends couldn't relate. Here I am and I lost my brother, but none of my friends had lost a brother or sister.

"I was looking for some type of comfort somewhere, but I had to do it on my own. I didn't want to go to my mom, so I just hung out with my friends. I remember seeing a brochure from Compassionate Friends about losing a child, but I wanted to see one about losing a brother. I wanted to know that I wasn't alone in my grief. I really wanted to find something that would help.

"I still felt very much loved at home, but I didn't want my grief to add to Mom's grief. I wanted to be strong for her. I felt my mom's grief was more important to deal with than my own. That was how I felt. I wanted to make sure she was okay, and that it wasn't about me. But I didn't realize I was fighting my grief. I had no idea but felt there was no outlet for the overwhelming feelings I had. I needed to hear that I would be okay. And I wanted proof of it somehow. I wanted to hear it from someone who had experienced it, made it through it, and came out okay.

"Still to this day, I meet new people and they ask me do you have any brothers and sisters. I have to take a pause and say, 'Yes, I have a brother in spirit,' and look up towards the sky with my hands out. 'He passed away when I was twenty.'

"I knew Betty was very ill and I distanced myself from Betty because I thought I would feel less when she passed away, but that didn't work. While she was ill and after she passed away, the panic attacks started. I always felt that if I ever was in a situation like this again, I would get the panic attacks again.

"I still don't know how I got through it. For months, I had panic attacks, and my blood pressure was up. Every day, I woke up and always my hands were in fists because I was so tightly wound. One morning, I woke up and I felt different. My hands weren't in fists anymore, and strangely, it was like a fog had lifted.

"Years later, when my husband, Russ, died, I vowed that I would let myself feel everything and let myself grieve and cry and allow myself to heal."

I tried to look up forums or organizations that could help with the loss of a sibling, but there still isn't one just for that. I discovered a lot of grief groups on Twitter that cover all loss. Look for one that appeals to you.

We did it. We finally made it through. But it took a few years for me to come out of my fog. I don't even remember those years well. But we made it though. You will, too. It isn't that the grief ever goes away entirely. It just sort of hibernates until deep contemplation brings it back again. It doesn't last long though, then it goes back to sleep. It's bittersweet when it happens. I like to think about Chad, but it still hurts. When I start to imagine him with a wife and children, I have to stop myself. Just STOP! Because that isn't a place where I can safely go.

I am very grateful that I had him for eighteen years, and then it was Jack's turn. I like to think of the two of them together because it brings me peace somehow.

So how did I cope with Chad's death? It was very hard, but I do believe that he went back to where we all came from in the first place. It isn't that easy. Even though I felt that way, the visceral loss of him was terrible. I did feel him with me, and was fortunate to have a wonderful Serbian friend of my mother's, Luba, come to me with a long-lasting candle that she told me to light and to keep lit until I lit another one. I wasn't to let it go out until I felt I was healing. It brought me great comfort, which is why I suggested it earlier in this book.

Luba was one of the most holy people I have ever met. She was like a nun, but way too earthy to be one. She was funny and naughty. But her spirit and contact with Father, Son and the Holy Ghost were like no other I know. When she turned eighty-one, she told me she felt eighteen again. She was full of fun and laughter and love. She died not long after Chad's death and finally went Home again where she belonged.

Chapter 13

My Sister Betty, Happy-Go-Lucky

When I was born, Betty hated me. She felt loved by our father Nick and worried that his attention now would be on me and taken away from her. She was eleven. But I must have grown on her, because she used to sing me to sleep every night, and she had a beautiful voice.

Millie and Betty created their own language probably so I wouldn't understand. They used to call each other "Chassie." Millie was always in Betty's life whether she wanted her to be or not. I think it was karma of some kind. I saw a picture of them together when they both were very young. In the picture, they both had one leg under them and one hanging down. Ironically, the legs they were sitting on were the ones they eventually lost.

When Betty found out she was pregnant at seventeen, Mom talked to her about having an abortion or giving up the baby for adoption. But when Vicki was born, we all fell in love with her. She was so beautiful, and I was enthralled. So up went the crib, and we all stayed in the same room together—Betty, Baba, me, and Vicki.

What a strange family we were. We would all live together, then Betty, the kids, and Baba would move away, then all of us would be living together again. Then Mom and I moved to Pomona, but after a few years, we were all back living together again.

Betty married Melvin Maule, and she and Vicki went to live with him in Lansing, Michigan. I missed her terribly. She had a difficult pregnancy with Steven and had a breech birth. She was torn apart inside from the birth and had to have a lot of stitches, but when she came home from the hospital, Mel insisted on having sex and raped her. She told me she sat in a tub of hot water and scrubbed herself with a wire brush. I don't know why she stayed with him. But she convinced him to return to California, and they lived with us when I was eleven. I think she wanted to learn a vocation and took secretarial classes. She was a wiz with numbers and math and eventually got a job working in finance.

Unfortunately, Mel was a scoundrel, and there wasn't a woman he met he didn't try to sleep with. He even threw me on the bed once and kissed me inappropriately when I was only eleven. I feared and hated him after that and never wanted to be alone with him. I didn't tell my sister because it would have hurt her.

One time, a woman came to our home. She was a regular customer of my mom's, and she was standing in the kitchen with Betty and me. Betty had a cast-iron pan in her hand and was making breakfast when Dottie told her how lucky she was to have such a virile husband, intimating that she had sex with Mel. My dear sister Betty told her that she better leave the kitchen immediately or she would be wearing that cast-iron skillet on her head.

When I turned thirteen, Betty lived in Torrance with Mel, Vicki, Steve, and Baba, and Millie and I would stay with them every summer, then go back and live with Mom. But Betty finally got a divorce, and we were all back together again. You can see why I moved around so much. We all did.

It was Betty who encouraged me to become a secretary. She told me to learn to take shorthand and type so I could get a good job. She told me if I didn't have a vocation, I would never do well. That advice was the best I could have ever received. I trained until my skills were excellent, and I had many lucrative executive secretarial jobs in my life because of it.

After I was graduated from high school, we were both employed by the air force in a civil service capacity. Betty would drive us to work, and absolutely every single day, we would approach this one street—I don't remember the name— and she would always ask me which way to turn. She had absolutely no sense of direction. She was such a character!

Betty was her own woman and didn't take suggestions easily from Mom. They were similar in one way and like water and oil in another. Betty went her own way, and some of what she did was pretty unsavory. She did what she needed to do to keep a roof over her head and feed her children.

She finally found her own true love, Lui Kaolalo, when she was in her thirties. Lui was a pure Hawaiian, and he played the slack-key guitar, sang like a dream, and did all the housework—he cooked and ironed and cleaned—while Betty worked. He had been a longshoreman when a girder fell on his ankle, crushing it, so Lui collected disability and didn't work. But he took my sister everywhere and calmly waited for her as she did her errands. They truly loved and were devoted to each other. When Lui was thirty-six, he developed a blood clot in his lung and suddenly died. Betty never looked for another man. Lui was it for her. She took his remains and moved to Hawaii, and there she stayed for twelve years.

I received a telephone call one evening after Betty had moved and was living in Hawaii, and Betty told me she was in unbelievable pain. She had been treated for an infected little toe, but the doctor didn't bother following up, and now she had to have it amputated. Unfortunately, by the time she called me, the pain had worked up her leg, and she couldn't stand it. The next thing I knew, her leg was being amputated from below the knee down. Jack had just recently died, Millie had lost her leg two months before that, and I just wasn't able to cope with anything more. I asked my Niece Vicki if she would go and take care of her mom, and she did.

As I mentioned earlier, I went to visit Betty in Hawaii about seven months later. When she met me at the airport, she greeted me standing upright. That evening, we all watched Princess Diana and Prince Charles get married on television.

About a year later, Betty got a settlement from a malpractice lawsuit. She called and wanted to come back to the mainland and stay with us, which is what she did. Millie followed a few months later. After a few months, they found a place close to us and moved there permanently. Betty worked with John and me in our business, and Millie stayed home. One day, I stopped by to see how Millie was doing and realized she had a stroke. Nothing she said made sense, and she could no longer read. Later on, she just stared in a dazed way. (In the chapter on Millie, I discussed what happened to her and how hard it was on all of us.)

After Mille went to stay in a nursing home for large-wound care, Betty moved in with us, and she was part of our family. Our family was just John, Chad, Betty, Nichole, and me, and we all looked after one another. Betty was having a very hard time with a wound in her leg. One time, her artery tore open, and blood gushed everywhere. She was standing up, and I heard her say, "Oh, oh." I pushed her down in her wheelchair, then to the bed, then shoved her from the wheelchair to her bed, lifted her leg up, and asked Nichole for something to make a tourniquet. While I tried to wrap gauze around her thigh, I asked Nichole to call 911. It was a close call. The doctor would only operate on Betty if she promised to stop smoking. Otherwise, she would lose the leg. The doctor performed an amazing surgery, and Betty kept her word and stopped smoking. Nichole had a very hard time dealing with what Betty was going through. Chad had recently died, and Nichole's panic attacks were terrible. Finally, she had to move out. She just couldn't live with us and heal herself.

Over time, we moved again, and Betty started to decline. She had been on oxygen during the day, but then had to go on it twenty-four hours a day, and then she was diagnosed with congestive heart failure. She would wheel herself to the door and open it just so she could breathe in fresh air. She wasn't eating, but her body weight went up because she was retaining water. She could no longer lift herself up from the toilet using only one leg, so we got her a portable wheelchair potty chair, but she wasn't eating or taking care of herself, and I was getting so upset. I felt that I wasn't a very good caretaker. I started to feel resentful, and then I had the epiphany that this was for me: Taking care of Betty was my challenge. Vicki had taken care of my mom; I was taking care of hers. I resolved to love her as much as I could. But the day came when I realized I couldn't help her. I didn't have the capability of washing her and making sure she was eating. At this point, she weighed well over 300 lbs and wasn't even eating.

I called San Diego Hospice to see if I could get some help. They were willing, but the doctor had to approve the care. When I called her doctor, he was out of town, and the doctor in charge insisted that she couldn't recommend hospice unless Betty came to see her. I asked her how I was supposed to get a 300 lb woman with one leg with an oxygen apparatus into a car to get her to the doctor. The doctor didn't care.

After calling hospice again, they told me to call an ambulance and notify the hospital that Betty could not return home because we couldn't take care of her. The lady at hospice told me they would have to put her in a convalescent home.

Betty and I had a very difficult conversation. Her greatest fear was to be put in a convalescent home, and here I was suggesting it. She didn't want it. I asked her how she thought I could take care of her, to make sure she was clean and fed. I was crying and at my wits end. I just didn't know what to do. She said, "Okay, do it." But with deep grief, I tell you that I felt I lost her love that day. I don't know if she ever forgave me.

Everything went as the woman at hospice said. The hospital turned her over to a nice convalescent hospital. She was in a room with another woman. But the day we visited, I heard her crying. She had messed herself and was embarrassed as the nurse was trying to take care of her. I was appalled. I asked if she was being treated by hospice and was told no. This is not what I wanted for her. This was not for her greater good.

John and I went to the doctor there and asked him why she wasn't receiving hospice care. He said we didn't understand; that if they put her on hospice, she would only last about two weeks because they would give her morphine and she would slowly pass away. I insisted he go with us to talk to her. I know she wanted the care. The doctor told her if he started hospice care, she would only live about two weeks. She responded, "Bless you, doctor." They started hospice care the next day. We all came to hug her and say good-bye. She was sitting up in bed and gave me a hug and said, "Good-bye, Sissy." How can that be? It is just too surreal. Betty died thirty-six hours after they gave her morphine.

When I came back to get her things, the nurse told me that she had one of the most beautiful passings they had ever witnessed.

Betty told them that her husband, Lui, was watching her in the doorway, and Betty started singing beautiful Hawaiian love songs to him. They all listened as she finally just went to sleep and let go. She told me all the nurses were crying.

We had a memorial at the beach. Her children Vicki and Steve, and John, Nichole, and I were all there as we sent her off with flowers in the water. We took her remains back to the funeral home to make arrangements for her to be let go in the ocean. But I know where she really is—somewhere in Hawaii with Lui.

I missed Betty a lot. But I was truly glad she was no longer suffering. It's very hard to see someone you love deteriorate slowly, then altogether. She wanted to die, to be with Lui again. She's free now, and I'm sure that's where she is; she's with him.

Chapter 14

My Nephew and His Demons

Stephen Maule was born when I was eleven. Betty, Mel, Steve, and Vicki all came from Lansing, Michigan to live with us for a while when Steve was a year old as Mel looked for work. Steve was a sweet baby, but when Betty left Mel a few years later, Mel never chose to have contact with his son, and I know that Steve felt abandoned without a father figure to guide him. We were, after all, a group of only women at that time. And Millie criticized Steve as she had criticized me when I was growing up.

By the time Steve was thirteen, he started sniffing glue and getting into trouble. Betty turned him over to the authorities to straighten him out. He was sent to a juvenile camp for over a year. He went to school but always was in trouble, so when he was seventeen, my sister's new husband, Lui, made him a bargain. Get beat up by Lui, who was a very large man, or go into the service. Steve chose the service, and he thrived there and even became a member of one of the 84th Airborne division parachute teams. Unfortunately, during one of the jumps, another parachute got too close to him and made his parachute collapse. Steve fell three stories to the ground. While he luckily survived, he had back problems the rest of his life from that fall, and he had to leave the service. Steve was stationed in Hawaii, and Betty moved there after Lui died to lay his ashes to rest.

When Steve got out of the service, he asked to stay with Jack and me until he found a job. That was fine with us, but Steve had his demons, and they were significant. He became an alcoholic and started using cocaine. He was with us for three months. He made money, but he didn't find his own place, so Jack gave him two weeks to find a new home. He moved out and disappeared from all of us for a while but would call around the holidays.

Steve also had a real problem with the truth. I think he created his own reality. I could never believe what he told me. There was probably a smidgen of truth in what he said, but that was all.

When my sisters moved back from Hawaii, Steve moved into the house with them. After Millie was hospitalized, I got a call from Betty. She said, "Cookie, do you love me?" I told her of course I did. She asked if she could live with me. I said, "Of course." When I asked her what had happened, she told me Steve was acting erratically, and she felt threatened. We picked her up that night. The next we heard, Steve had beaten up someone quite badly at a bar and was arrested for assault and battery. He was sentenced to eighteen months in jail and had to attend AAA meetings.

He came out sober and stayed sober for twelve years. He had a good job and was going to junior college and doing well, if I could believe what he said. He was able to buy a home on the VA bill, and we were all happy for him. He even found a woman to love and got married.

Unfortunately, he started drinking again shortly after he married. Things went from bad to worse, and his wife divorced him a year later. He was very self-destructive during that time. I told him that I would take him to the VA for alcohol treatment and that I would pick him up. But he called me the day he was supposed to go and said he just couldn't do it. Sometimes, we have to make a decision for our own sanity and safety. I told him that I couldn't be part of his life until he chose to let go of the alcohol. Betty had died. Vicki was in Texas, and he didn't have any family other than me and Nichole. But I couldn't subject my family to an unstable alcoholic. It was a difficult stand for me to take, but I felt there was no choice.

We all lost track of him over the years. Vicki tried to find him, but couldn't. I knew he lived in San Diego, but that was all.

One day I got a call from Vicki. She told me that a hospital had called to tell her that Steve had died. He had congestive heart failure and was in a wheelchair. She was listed as the next of kin. He had been living in a communal rooming house. He had one room and a bathroom. So we went there to settle his affairs. I knew so little about him by then, but I found his phone and called those listed to tell them he had passed away.

We were only going to have a small memorial service for him, but by making those phone calls, we found that Steve had created an "alternate" life. He had a favorite bar he preferred, and everyone there loved him. He had told them that he was a retired professor from UCSD, that his wife had died in an automobile accident, and that he had no family left. "They" had all lived in Hawaii.

There was a very pleasant woman with a young boy who Steve had befriended. She worked at the restaurant-bar, and she was very fond of Steve. He told her that he had put her on his insurance policy in case he died. Unfortunately, that was a lie, too.

I made all the arrangements for a VA funeral, and all the people from the bar attended and said lovely things about Steve. They thought he was a great guy and would miss him. It was a total surprise to them that he had an aunt (me) who lived in San Diego when they all thought he was alone. It was a very nice tribute with Taps playing. I wanted to keep his fantasy alive for them. It was my last gift to him.

In retrospect, I think that Steve made up a fantasy life and actually believed it. He was a pathological liar. If his made-up life brought him comfort, I'm all for it. When we struggle with major issues in life that we can't face, we do things and make decisions to make our lives work and be worthwhile. Steve was worthwhile to all of those people. He'd always been worthwhile to me and his sister, we just couldn't help him.

It takes so much courage to face our demons and overcome drug and alcohol addiction. I take my hat off to those who can. It must be a difficult, even impossible road to find recovery. But many people can and do. There are so many places one can find help, but taking those steps, that's the issue.

Chapter 15

Life-after-Life Experiences

Hopefully, I won't lose too many of you reading this, but I could not write this book without talking about the unusual experiences I've had after the loss of a loved one.

I know that many people talk to their loved ones who have passed away or see them in a chair or at the foot of a bed or smell flowers or have a sense of them being present. Whether it is real or imagined, these experiences bring a peace that defies reason. You may have dreams about your loved ones. If you remember the dreams, I believe you were definitely visited.

When my brother-in-law, Lui, died, I was standing in front of some books with very heavy bookends on both sides, and suddenly all the books were pushed aside and tumbled over.

After my mom passed away, I was standing at my bathroom sink. Right over the counter was a large, round, hanging globe, and it suddenly just broke. Nothing touched it, but right in front of me, it just cracked into pieces.

I was lying in bed and felt a sharp tug on the sheet as though it were being pulled off me. This happened just after Jack died.

But things really revved up after Chad died. It was as though he were playing with us and doing everything to say, "I'm still here." There was so much activity that even my friends noticed it.

I gave a party for a group I belonged to, and the patio table was set with champagne glasses and filled with food. I was in the kitchen and heard a loud "ting." The kitchen wasn't anywhere near the patio. My girlfriend brought me a champagne glass that had broken into two pieces, the globe from the stem. She said, "Your son is busy tonight." The glass was just sitting there, then broke right in front of the people on the patio. They all saw it happen.

Once, when I went to take a shower, I turned the light on and let the water in the shower run to get warm and stepped out of the bathroom for a moment. I heard a loud "click," and the light went off.

Nichole was in the bathroom, and her blow dryer turned on all by itself. She quickly hit the off button, and it turned right back on. The she got scared and pulled the plug from the socket. Right after that, she was sad that she had broken the connection.

At the office, we found the cord of the microwave tied in a knot, and the lights turned on and off there as well. There was no reason for any of it.

Chad had created a beautiful, stained-glass clock, and it was hanging on a wall even though the batteries hadn't worked for a while. My niece, Vicki, came to visit and stayed in his room, and the clock started working again.

We had a pull-out door between rooms that never locked. I didn't think it had a lock on it. My landlord said it didn't lock, but it did, often. We had to turn a screw to open it.

There were some extremely memorable times that just defy logic. I had gone into Chad's room where we had a bookshelf library, and I took down a book and went back into my bedroom to sit in my reading chair. I read for a while and looked down for some reason. I was wearing a nylon nightie. You know how slippery they are. Well, the nightie had been rolled up to my midthighs. I unrolled it down and out came a Blaupunkt plug. Chad worked with car stereos, and the plug was from a Blaupunkt radio. How can you explain it? I can't. I put that memento in my memory scrapbook.

It was Mother's Day, just a month after Chad's death, and I needed a match to light a 7-day candle. It suddenly occurred to me that since Chad was a smoker, he might have matches in his box of treasures that I had discovered. I opened the box and sure enough, there was a matchbook. I opened it to light the candle, and the entire inner part of the matchbook was about Mother's Day. Did I get the thought to look in that box from him? Or did it just materialize somehow? I don't know. But I loved the message.

Another time, I was watching TV, and my purse was on top of

it. As I was looking at the TV, the handle of the purse fell down in front of it. I remember thinking that if the handle moved, I would know it was from Chad. As I looked, the handle started to wind around. I got goose bumps. He did everything to send us a message that life continues…just not in the corporeal form.

And, finally, a really weird event happened when my husband John, Betty, and I were finishing dinner one night. We were all seated at the table in an open concept area where the living room is next to us. We heard a noise, and all of us watched as an empty Diet Coke can lifted itself up from a side table and sailed over an ottoman to land on the floor. It must have flown five feet. The can had been sitting there since the night before. So, how can that happen? None of us tried to rationalize it, but just accepted it as a gift.

I would love to hear from others about their experiences. Most people don't share them because they're afraid other people will think less of them or think that in their grief, they are imagining things.

Many people have experiences of seeing or feeling their loved ones contact them from the other side. I call it the "gift" that comes with grief. We seem to be closer to that psychic ceiling that divides the living from those gone from this life.

So many of us shut down this possibility of contact from our loved ones because of our beliefs, whether religious or otherwise, or because we are naturally skeptical or cynical. I say, be open. Let go of your beliefs and just let happen whatever may or may not happen. Don't judge it. If you are fortunate enough to experience these events, you will feel very peaceful and believe, as I do now, that there is life after death.

My journey continues as I write this book. I am happy and look forward to what is next in my life. Writing and publishing this book has been a challenge all on its own, but I enjoyed the process. My journey always seems to be changing anyway no matter what I do. My wish for you is to find peace and joy again and to make it through the rain. Please look at my website, lenayrogus.com, to download the free Guilt Release Hypnosis and see my blog as well. I would love to hear from you.

And just a quick update for those of you who may wonder about how Nichole is doing. I'm happy to say she recently got engaged to a wonderful man, Chuck Toledo, who already calls me Mom. The wedding will be this summer.

I shall leave you with one last thought. I had a dream. Chad was standing with two people grooming him. I looked up and saw that he had beautiful, golden wings.

I said, "Chad, you're an angel."

He gently said, "I know, Mom."

Marie Lenay Rogus is a Hypnotherapist, Stress Management Consultant and speaker and producer of hypnosis downloads on her website, she is a San Diego Hospice trained bereavement group facilitator and a Childbirth Educator with additional certification in EFT and Hypnoanesthesia. Lenay is also an entrepreneur and co-founder of Peripheral Electronics, Inc., which was sold to a publically held company. Prior to Peripheral, her career was in the motion picture industry, where she was a production coordinator and paralegal.

If you liked this book please leave a review on Amazon. You can also email me at lenay.rogus@gmail.com. It would be my privilege to hear your stories as well.

You can keep in touch using the following links:

> Email: lenay@griefcomfortguide.com
> Website: http://griefcomfortguide.com
> My blog is linked to my website.
> https://www.facebook.com/lenay.rogus
> https://facebook.com/griefcomfort
> https://twitter.com/GriefComfort

46806994R00071

Made in the USA
San Bernardino, CA
15 March 2017